Heroes and Villains

The astounding untold story of the founders of Cascade Brewery

By Gregory Jefferys

Bachelor of Arts; University of Queensland
Diploma of Education; University of Queensland
Master of History University of Tasmania

J.A.G. Publications

i

Published by:
J.A.G Publications
P.O. Box 217 Woodbridge
Tasmania
Australia 7162

"Heroes and Villains"

By Greg Jefferys

ISBN **978-0-646-91046-8**

Front and back covers by Greg Jefferys, front cover using
painting of Cascade Brewery by Haughton Forrest (circa 1880)
with portrait of Peter Degraves from family collection of Tony
Fleetwood Wilson (artist unknown) and portrait of Persian
Crown Prince Abbas Mirza (circa 1830 artist unknown).

Printed in China
By Aomeiya Printing Co.Ltd.
info@aomeiya-printing.com

Foreword

This story had its origins in my Master's thesis, which originally began as a study of the ship *Hope,* her buried treasure legend and the various people who sailed on her however as I investigated the lives of Hugh Macintosh and Peter Degraves, who were responsible for bringing the *Hope* to Hobart and founding the Cascade Brewery, I found such an intriguing story that I changed the topic of my thesis to focus on the lives of these two amazing men whose story, until now, has remained largely untold.

Peter Degraves is, today, primarily remembered as the founder of the Cascade Brewery and as one of Tasmania's first industrial entrepreneurs. It is commonly believed that within only fifteen years of his arrival in Hobart in 1824, Degraves was solely responsible for building a timber mill, a flour mill, a brewery, a ship building yard, a large farm and a theatre. All of these enterprises were financially successful, while two of them, the brewery and the theatre, are still operating today, almost 200 years later.

Despite these achievements there is little in the existing literature that deals in any detail with the 46 years of Degraves' life prior to his arrival in Hobart Town and the few details of that period that do exist are generally vague with little or no documentary support other than material that Peter Degraves himself wrote.

As I began to examine Degraves' pre-colonial life I found that the reason for the historic vagueness was that most of the accepted history of Degraves' early life was completely false and that there was a large body of information regarding his early life that Degraves had deliberately hidden and which until now had remained undiscovered. For example the fact that he had been a bankrupt for most of the first decade of the 19th century and had been imprisoned for a massive theft in 1810-11. These new discoveries paint a very different and more complete picture of Degraves the man, a man of genius who was utterly ruthless; a man of enormous energy who could successfully turn his mind to almost any task but who desperately sought to obscure the scandals of his past. This new material also provide insights that explain the forces that drove Degraves to succeed at any cost while demonstrating the brilliance of a man who, despite his claims to the contrary, had no formal training or genuine expertise in any of the fields in which he claimed to be an authority.

In contrast to Peter Degraves Major Hugh Macintosh is rarely remembered in his own right and occurs almost as an afterthought when the history of the Cascade Brewery or Peter Degraves is mentioned. Apart from being Degraves' brother-in-law it is sometimes recalled that the two men were partners in the Cascade's foundation and expansion. It is also occasionally noted that Macintosh was an ex-officer of the Honourable East India Company's Army and that he was the co-owner of the ship *Hope,* which brought him, Degraves, their families, workers and equipment to Hobart. Beyond these small details I found almost nothing existed describing the life of Hugh Macintosh. However despite his present historic obscurity I discovered that Macintosh was centrally and closely involved with a number of important historic events and personages in England, India, Persia and Australia. Macintosh was an educated and highly cultured man who was also a courageous and battle hardened soldier. He painted, played the violin and spoke at least five languages; he had close relationships with the Crown Prince of Persia, the Duke of Wellington and the family of Lord Hobart as well as being the patron of Henry Savery who would not have written Australia's first novel, *Quintus Servington*, without the support of Hugh Macintosh. The more I learned of the life of Hugh Macintosh the more compelled I felt to correct the historic record by telling the true story of the events that led to the creation of the Cascade Brewery and its success.

The focus of this book is primarily on the period in the lives of Macintosh and Degraves prior to their arrival in Hobart, providing an overview of the lives of these two interesting men and the very different worlds they inhabited. In order to make the story more readable and interesting I have added a lot more material related to the personal lives of the main characters and included more images than were in my thesis. For the same reason I have also removed a lot of the footnotes and referencing that was in the thesis whilst retaining the original bibliography. For anyone who is particularly interested in the source of a piece of information the fully referenced thesis is available on-line from 'e prints' at the University of Tasmania.

Acknowledgements

Thanks to all people who have helped me with this work. In particular I would like to thank Prof. Hamish Maxwell-Stewart for his advice; John Owen and Jan Jefferys for their editorial input and Anne Blythe for her insights into the life of Sophia Degraves, the connection between Hugh Macintosh and Henry Savery and the existence of William Hugh Macintosh. I also would like to thank Tony Fleetwood Wilson, a descendant of both Degraves and Macintosh, for giving me access to his family archives and the results of his extensive research and for assisting me with my research in London. Without Tony's assistance many of the interesting personal insights into the lives of his ancestors would have remained undiscovered.

Contents

Introduction: p. viii

Section One: Peter Degraves, Hero or Villain?

Chapter 1 Hero of Industry   p. 1
Chapter 2 The Sins of the Father   p.6
Chapter 3 Bankrupt, Businessman and Burglar p.31
Chapter 4 Highland Exile   p.47

Section Two: Hugh Macintosh, the Honourable Mutineer

Chapter 5: The Company Cadet   p.61
Chapter 6: Madras and Mysore   p.75
Chapter 7: Siege of Seringapatam   p.88
Chapter 8: Marriage and Mutiny   p.111
Chapter 9: Serving the Shah   p.128

Section Three: The *Hope* and on to Hobart

Chapter 10: The Colonial Ship *Hope*   p.139
Chapter 11: Refitting and Finances   p.150
Chapter 12: The Hopeful Emigrants   p.160
Chapter 13: Ramsgate Harbour to Hobart   p.178
Chapter 14: The Degraves Empire   p.199

Conclusion: A Deceptive Distance   p.208
Appendix 1. The Bruny Island Treasure   p. 218
Bibliography: p.227

List of Illustrations:

Peter Degraves	p. 1
Doctor Pierre Degravers	p. 6
Red Lion Square, Soho	p. 13
Deacon Brodie	p. 21
Slave Ship Surgeon	p. 28
Kings Bench Prison	p. 45
Mary Stewart Mackenzie	p. 51
Harrow School	p. 62
East India Company ship	p. 72
Fort St George Madras	p. 75
Madras Native Infantry Officer	p. 76
Hyder Ali	p. 78
Captain David Baird	p. 80
Young Tipu Sultan	p. 82
Madras Native Infantry	p. 87
Siege of Seringapatam (map)	p. 88
Tipu Sultan	p. 89
Storming the Breech Seringapatam	p. 95
General Arthur Wellesley	p. 101
Famine Struck Villagers	p. 103
Battle of Assaye (map)	p. 105
Charging the Marathas Cannon Line	p. 106
Fortress Gawilghur	p. 108
William Nicholson (by S. Drummond)	p. 113
Mary Wollstonecraft	p. 115
Fortress of Chittaldroog	p. 116
Sir George Barlow	p. 123
The Dragoons	p. 125
Persia's Crown Prince	p. 128
A Persian Soldier	p. 133
Erivan's Palace of Mirrors	p. 134
Crown Prince Abbas Mirza	p. 135
An early Clipper Ship	p. 139
The Ship Worm (teredo worm)	p. 144

Limehouse Canal in London   p. 149
Mary Reibey   p. 152
Ratcliffe Highway   p. 153
Macintosh & Degraves Silver Shilling   p. 156
John Wesley   p. 161
Ship's Graveyard Goodwin Sands   p. 170
Sarah Benson Walker   p. 171
Mary Reibey's Sydney Home   p. 180
Hobart's Giant Gum Trees   p. 185
Cascade Mill's Waterwheel   p. 186
Governor Arthur   p. 187
Hobart Town circa 1840   p. 190
Cascade Brewery (H. Forrest)   p. 199
Henry Degraves   p. 204
Deborah Hope Degraves   p. 206

Introduction

The first few decades of Australian history are dotted with stories of people whose energy and vision created the structures and institutions around which Australia's economy, culture and legends would grow. Some of these people have been remembered as heroes and others have been remembered as villains and yet others have simply been forgotten. The stories that surround many of these characters have developed into mythologies that have helped perpetuate the "pioneer" traditions associated with early colonial Australia although in some cases these myths bare little resemblance to the historical facts of their subject's lives.[1] In many cases these mythologies have been perpetuated, largely unchallenged, to the present day in order to foster some sense of connectedness between present day institutions and Australia's limited antiquity.[2] Hidden amongst these pioneer "heroes" there are persons who arguably made equal, or even greater, contributions to early Australian social, cultural or economic development, but who have had their life stories and achievements ignored.[3] In the early years of Hobart Town two men, Hugh Macintosh and his brother-in-law, Peter Degraves, made a huge impact on the economic and cultural development of the young colony. Both men were possessed of the vision and the drive necessary to bring their dreams into reality, but whilst Peter Degraves is today lauded as an enterprising colonial industrialist and entrepreneurial hero, Hugh Macintosh is all but forgotten.[4]

Peter Degraves is primarily remembered as the founder of the Cascade Breweries and as one of Tasmania's first industrial

---

[1] J. Hirst *Sense and Nonsense in Australian History* (Melbourne)2005

[2] E. Hobsbawm 'Inventing Traditions' *The Invention of Traditions* ed. E. Hobsbawm (Cambridge) 1983 pp. 3-14

[3] Many of these "invisible" heroes were women, whose work and bravery was rarely recorded but without whose support our well known male pioneer heroes could never have achieved the successes to which they lay claim.

[4] M. Bingham *Cascade: A Taste of History* (Hobart)1991 p.3

entrepreneurs, an industrial pioneer, and as such fits neatly into Australia's pioneer traditions. [5] It is commonly, though incorrectly, believed that within just fifteen years of his arrival in Hobart in 1824, Degraves had built a timber mill, a flour mill, a brewery, a shipbuilding yard and a theatre. All of these enterprises were financially successful, while two of them, the Cascade Brewery and Hobart's Theatre Royal, are still in operation today, almost 200 years later.

Degraves also created an industrial laboratory at the Cascades complex where he worked on numerous projects, including testing various native Tasmanian tree barks for use in the British cloth dyeing industry and growing yeast for his brewery and for Hobart's bakers.[6] Apart from his successful business enterprises, Peter Degraves is also known to have unsuccessfully attempted a number of other ambitious projects.[7] These included designing a water reticulation system to supply all of Hobart with running water, and a plan for a new Hobart prison, which would have included a treadmill that he considered to be of a more efficient design than anything else then in use. Perhaps not surprisingly he asked the authorities to keep secret his treadmill design, fearing retribution if certain people discovered he had designed the instrument of their torture.

These industrial/entrepreneurial feats are documented in a range of existing histories of Degraves' life written over the past one hundred years. These all tell a similar story about a multi-talented entrepreneur and "model English gentleman" who migrated to Van Diemen's Land to found what would become a vast business empire in a fledgling British colony on the outer

---

[5] B. Hooper *Peter Degraves, Pioneer Industrialist,* Honours Dissertation University of Tasmania 1969

[6] E. Markham *Voyage to Van Dieman's Land, aboard the ship Warrior* (London)1834 pp. 11-13

[7] G. Lloyd *Thirty Three Years in Tasmania and Victoria* (London) 1862

fringes of the civilised world. In these histories Degraves is variously portrayed as a skilled architect, engineer, mathematician, lawyer, surveyor and a "pioneer industrialist" who, in his middle life, came to Hobart Town from Britain and flourished despite the obstacles presented by the colonial environment.[8] Yet there is little in the existing literature that deals in any detail with the 46 years of Degraves' life prior to his arrival in Hobart Town and what few details there are regarding that period are brief and vague with little or no documentary support other than what Degraves himself had provided. A close examination of Degraves' pre-colonial life quickly shows the reason for this brevity and vagueness, for most of what is accepted as the history of Degraves' early life is based either on exaggeration or deliberate falsehood. Further, there are many omitted details which until now have remained undiscovered. This new evidence paints a very different, if somewhat more complete, picture of Degraves the man: a man of undoubted genius but who was also utterly ruthless. He was a man who could turn his mind to almost any challenge and who was desperate to advance himself socially, though to achieve this he had to hide the scandals of his past and had no compunctions about lying to do so. Ultimately Degraves would use distance and the relative isolation afforded by Britain's colonial empire to reinvent himself, a tactic that was used, not infrequently, by other persons with similarly sullied reputations.[9] The new discoveries presented in this book also provide insights that help explain what drove Degraves to succeed at any cost while demonstrating the brilliance of a man who, while he had no formal training or genuine expertise in any of the fields in which he falsely claimed to be a leading authority, was nevertheless able to turn his hand to an impressive array of ventures.

---

[8] C. Allport *The Degraves Centenary* 1924
[9] K. McKenzie *Scandal in the Colonies* (Sydney) 2004

In contrast to Peter Degraves, Major Hugh Macintosh is rarely remembered in his own right although his name is sometimes mentioned in relation to the history of the Cascades Brewery.[10] Usually, however, this is only to record that he was Degraves' brother-in-law and that he was, somehow, a partner in the foundation of the Cascades. It is also occasionally noted that Macintosh had been an officer of the Honourable East India Company's Madras army and, sometimes, that he was the co-owner of the ship *Hope,* which brought him, Degraves, their workers, families and equipment to Hobart. Beyond these small details, however, almost nothing exists describing the rich and exciting life of Hugh Macintosh. This is particularly surprising given his critical role in the establishment and continuance of what was to become known as the "Degraves' Empire". Yet, despite his present historical obscurity, Macintosh was centrally involved with a number of important events and personages in England, India, Persia and Australia. There is no clear reason why his history has been ignored other than that, whilst both he and Degraves arrived in Hobart on the threshold of a defining "boom" period in the young colony's development, Macintosh had the misfortune to die twenty years earlier than Degraves.

This "boom" period, in which Degraves and Macintosh were fundamentally involved, affected all areas of endeavour in Van Diemen's Land, but was particularly obvious in agriculture and the whaling and sealing industries. It was a time when Hobart changed from being primarily a convict settlement to a place of industry and enterprise. From the mid 1820s onward Van Diemen's Land increasingly became an internationally connected place and Hobart, with its famous harbour, a busy hub for the southern ocean whaling and sealing industries, which the two men were able to benefit from.[11] The ship *Hope,* which Macintosh and Degraves owned and which brought them

---

[10] B. Hooper *Peter Degraves, Pioneer Industrialist,* 1969
[11] R Hartwell *The economic development of Van Diemen's Land* 1953

to Hobart, was to play an important role in the colony's maritime history. In fact this work originally began as a study on the ship *Hope* however as the research progressed it became apparent that it was the story of the ship's owners that needed to be told. For this was a period in which Van Diemen's Land was much talked about in Britain as a colony with great prospects and a place where migrants, particularly those with capital, might make a new life for themselves and their families.[12] It was clear that the story of these two men, and the journey through life that ultimately bought them to Hobart, provided profound insights into the circumstances and processes which led to people making the momentous decision to emigrate to the Australian colonies.

It was fortunate that the research for this thesis began in a period when vast amounts of archival material were being digitalised and placed on the internet. It was through these digital resources, accessible through the university's databases or through publicly accessible sites, such as Google Books, that I was able to discover that which had previously been hidden or lost.

Both Degraves and Macintosh presented unique challenges in on-line searching as both surnames had multiple spelling options. For example Macintosh is frequently spelt as McIntosh, Mackintosh or even Mac Intosh, whilst Degraves has been spelt De Graves, Degreaves, Degravers and Degrave. Hugh Macintosh was a particularly interesting challenge because the founder of the Apple/Macintosh computer empire was also named Hugh Macintosh, meaning any internet search specifically focused on that name produced hundreds of millions of hits. These factors forced the development of quite sophisticated searching techniques.

---

[12] M. Bingham *Cascade: a taste of history.*(Hobart) 1991: S. Rickard *Lifelines from Calcutta* 2003

Those difficulties aside, the digitalisation of archival records meant that it was possible to search through tens of thousands of pages of text in minutes, a task which would have taken years for a researcher even in the recent past. It is the digitalisation of historic records that made this possible and I particularly thank Google for making so many resources accessible to the general public.

The first section of this book will explore the early life of Peter Degraves, from his childhood up to his first abortive attempt to voyage to Van Diemen's Land aboard the *Hope* in October 1821. The second section will examine the life of Hugh Macintosh, a man with a past that was even more colourful and intriguing than that of Degraves. The third section will examine the history of the ship *Hope*, a typical colonial vessel of its time, the acquisition of which marked a turning point in the lives of Macintosh and Degraves. This section will also seek to unpick the complex web of competing stories which surround the first, unsuccessful, attempt by Macintosh and Degraves to sail the *Hope* to Van Diemen's Land. In doing so it will examine the controversial conflict between the two men and their Wesleyan passengers and what this conflict tells us about Macintosh and Degraves and the undercurrents of social change that were beginning to swirl through the British world. [13] It will also explore the background to the eventually successful voyage of 1823-24. The conclusion will also look at the process by which Degraves and Macintosh were able to reinvent themselves in Van Diemen's Land. It will examine how both men were able to turn the long delays in communications created by the "tyranny of distance" to their advantage by subtly changing key elements of their identities. [14] The conclusion will also explore the histories and mythologies surrounding these two men and the extent to which these can be used to examine identity, history

---

[13] K. McKenzie *A Swindler's Progress* (Sydney) 2010 pp. 293-298

[14] G. Blainey *The Tyranny of Distance* 1966

and the invention of tradition in a colonial setting.[15] Also, because of the public interest, there is included in the appendix an extensive examination of the legend of the *Hope's* lost treasure.

[15] E. Hobsbawm 'Inventing Traditions' *The Invention of Traditions* 1983

Section One: Peter Degraves, Hero or Villain?

Figure 1: Peter Degraves circa 1850 aged in his late 60's

Chapter 1: Hero of Industry

Hobart Courier: Monday 3 January 1853 page 3.

Obituary : THE LATE MR. P. DEGRAVES:- Our obituary of this day contains the announcement of the decease of the late Peter Degraves, Esq. Mr. Degraves arrived about 28 years ago in a vessel called the Hope, the joint property of himself and Major Mackintosh. His family were in a highly respectable position, of French extraction, Mr. Degraves being the son of an eminent medical practitioner for very many years resident in Dover, and brother of Colonel Degraves, lately deceased at Madras. Mr. Degraves was during a portion of his early life with the celebrated engineer Rennie. The deceased was well known as the proprietor of the extensive brewery and steam sawmills at the Cascades. His career as a colonist has been very successful: he was highly and deservedly esteemed, and leaves a large family resident in the colony.

Peter Degraves arrived in Hobart Town in 1824 with a steam engine, a saw mill and a corn mill, which he had brought out from England on board the *Hope*.[1] There was a significant demand for sawn timber in the young colony and also in Britain, so Degraves' first action was to set up the machinery of the sawmilling plant, which he soon extended to include a flour mill. As the story has it, when he arrived in the colony Degraves' engineering eye immediately saw that water power, freely available from the fast-flowing streams that ran down the steep slopes of Mount Wellington, would be more efficient and cost effective than a steam engine. He thus built his mill on the banks of the Hobart Rivulet where it joined with the Guy Fawkes Rivulet at a place called the Cascades using the skills of the tradesmen he had brought out with him to convert the mill's drive mechanisms from steam to water. To utilise the waters more effectively Degraves built dams across the rivulet. In the short term this was not a problem for the pioneering entrepreneur or anyone else; later, as Hobart's population grew it would become a bone of contention for those who lived downstream who came to see his control of the Hobart Rivulet's headwaters as a significant threat. The story goes that in 1832, after his release from five years in the Hobart debtor's prison, Degraves added a brewery to his Cascades domain—again utilising the clear, clean waters of the Hobart Rivulet.

After 1832 Degraves consolidated his base at the Cascades then rapidly expanded his business empire to include shipbuilding yards at Battery Point and extensive farmlands. By the end of the 1830s he had also designed, built and, by a circuitous route,

[1] B. Hooper *Peter Degraves Pioneer Industrialist* 1969 pp. 1-3

come to own Hobart's Theatre Royal, now Australia's oldest still operating theatre.

It has been claimed that by the end of the 1830s Degraves was one of the richest men in Australia (he is reported to have had an annual income of around £100,000 at a time when a skilled worker's wage was around £50 per annum).[2] When he died at the end of December 1852 a few days after his 74th birthday, his family was well poised to reap an even greater fortune by supplying the Victorian Gold Rush with flour, beer and timber.

In 1924, a booklet was published to celebrate the centenary of the Cascades Brewery (although the brewery did not actually begin operations until late 1832). Its first chapter was entitled *"The Degraves Centenary"* and was dedicated to Degraves and the dynasty he founded. The author, Cecil Allport, called for the name of Peter Degraves to "ever occupy a prominent place" amongst the captains of Australian enterprise and industry.[3] In addition to being an expert engineer, Allport says Degraves was:

> "… an architect of no mean order and also an able draughtsman. He had, moreover, a knowledge of surveying… and was an experienced mathematician well versed in the science of Algebra… an authority on water boring."

In her 1969 Honours dissertation Beverly Hooper reasonably calls Degraves a "pioneer industrialist" but in another detailed history of Peter Degraves given in a book entitled *Cascade: a taste of history* Degraves moves from being a pioneer to a hero. This work, sponsored by the Cascade Brewery and authored by Tasmanian journalist Mike Bingham in 1991, opens with the words:

---

[2] M. Reid-McIlreavy *Degraves, P. Australian Dictionary of Biography* 1966
[3] Allport's family members were peers of the Degraves family.

"Australians have not always recognised their country's true heroes and achievers despite professing admiration for individuals who dare to have a go, to challenge the odds and the system, and to follow a dream whatever the setbacks. It is therefore perhaps fortunate that Peter Degraves built his own memorials."

It is true, as Bingham implies above, that Degraves was largely forgotten by the Australian public for much of the 20th century. But in their attempts to write a history for Peter Degraves, and to promote him as a forgotten hero, his "official" biographers do not appear to wonder why he was forgotten. They skip over the fact that Degraves spent five of his first seven years in Van Diemen's Land in debtor's prison and that he was generally disliked by a large portion of Hobart's population. Likewise they gloss over or ignore the controversy that saw Degraves arrested and imprisoned when he first attempted to leave England for Hobart on the *Hope* in 1821 and there is no mention of the fact that he was bankrupted in 1807 and then imprisoned for theft in 1810.[4] Nor is there any mention of the well-documented suffering he directly inflicted on the hungry men, women and children crammed on board the overloaded *Hope,* or of his speculation with his passenger's fare money on London's short-term money market, or the fact that the fare money was not returned to the passengers after the *Hope* was seized by the Authorities in Royal Ramsgate Harbour for being unseaworthy and overcrowded.[5]

Indeed not only did Peter Degraves "build his own memorials", as Bingham puts it, he also built his own history—a history he passed down through his family, his friends and his letters; upon

---

[4] U.K National Archives HO 47/45/3
[5] S. Benson-Walker *Reminiscences of the Life* (Hobart) 1884 pp. 6-7

which his biographers have been forced to rely where primary and other documentary sources did not exist or were inaccessible. So who was the real Peter Degraves? To paraphrase Jane Austen in *Pride and Prejudice* "Who was his father? Who were his brothers and sisters?" and what did he really do with his life before he sailed to Van Diemen's Land?[6]

---

[6] Jane Austen in her work *Pride and Prejudice,* emphasises the importance placed on pedigree and family connections in early 19th century England in a dialog between the aristocrat, Lady Catherine de Bourgh, and Elizabeth Bennet, a Gentleman's daughter, this notion of pedigree and family connections was an important factor in Degraves' life.

Chapter Two: The Sins of the Father; Dr. Pierre De Gravers

Figure 2: Degraves' father Dr Pierre Degravers, 1776, before he moved from France to London. The books shown open in this image are the first, French edition of his book on eye surgery, which he later translated into English.

The history of Peter Degraves' life before he arrived in Hobart Town in 1824 has relied almost exclusively on Degraves' own rendition of his history, either through stories he told to his peers or from a number of letters and memorials written by Degraves, mostly from prison either in England or Hobart.[7] These letters were generally written to promote himself or his case in some form of legal dispute and are now mostly preserved in the Tasmanian State Archives.

Because these documents represented the bulk of the information on Degraves' pre-Hobart life available to his official biographers they were more or less forced to rely on their subject's own rendition of his history. However with the recent improvements of internet-based archival searching aids and the digitalisation of historic records in Australia and overseas it has now become possible to apply a more critical eye to Degraves' numerous and extensive claims of his many, supposed, achievements. The most important of these was that prior to arriving in Hobart he was a wealthy, highly respected and successful member of English society who became a victim of the times when he lost his vast fortune during the Napoleonic Wars as a result of the machinations of Bonaparte the tyrant—a claim clearly designed to extract sympathy in the post-war period.[8] There is also an inference in *Cassell's Picturesque Australasia* (1889) that Degraves was actually a member of the French nobility, with one website today claiming that he was the son of the Count Francis Louis De Grave (born: 1726) and English woman, Anne Jones.

As with much else, the sole documentary evidence that he had lost a fortune is contained in the letters and memorials Degraves wrote to Lieutenant Governor Arthur from Hobart gaol between 1826 and 1831, embroidered and supported by stories he told

---

[7] Tasmanian Archives, *Bonwick Transcripts*, Box 13, pp. 6272-6279
[8] Morris E. *Cassell's Picturesque Australasia* (London) 1889 p.147

guests around the dinner table after his release from prison.[9] Within the various versions of his tale Degraves claims that he once owned a number of factories in England (Hooper says four) employing three or four thousand workers, and that he had personally been worth more than one million pounds, which in today's money would have made him almost a billionaire. The facts are very different. Between 1803 and 1805 Degraves owned, in partnership with three other people, including his maternal aunt, a small cotton mill in Manchester—a business which was dissolved in late 1805 after existing for less than three years.[10] His next business venture was as a "warehouse man, dealer, and chapman"; also a partnership. A 'chapman' was a travelling salesman and in this role Degraves used his persuasive nature to sell, wholesale, various fabrics and other such things in the 'rag trade'. This business ended when Degraves was declared bankrupt in 1807—a bankruptcy he was not discharged from until at least 1809, if ever.[11] Indeed he never owned any large factories and probably never employed more than a couple of dozen workers, if that.

Issues of debt, bankruptcy and falsehood followed Degraves through most of his life and it was a recurring theme in his personal narrative that he portrayed himself as the victim of other people's machinations, conspiracies or generally malevolent acts. It is, however, a perspective that does not stand up to a close scrutiny, although it might be argued that Degraves' tendency to see himself as a perpetual victim had its psychological origins in his relationship (or perhaps more accurately, lack of a relationship) with his father, Dr. Peter Degravers.

---

[9] E. Markham *Voyage to Van Dieman's Land* (London) 1834 pp. 13-16
[10] *London Gazette* June 1805 p.808
[11] *London Gazette* February 1808 p. 189

All of Peter Degraves' official histories tell a story of his early life similar to the summary in his obituary. All generally agree that he was born in 1778 into the family of an eminent French medical doctor who had married an English woman and that he lived his early life in Dover. The exception is Edward E. Morris who, in *Cassell's Picturesque Australasia,* states that Peter Degraves was "A native of France, driven thence by the terrors of the Revolution" who took refuge in England and became a "naturalised subject". This claim is distinctly odd since the French Revolution did not begin until 1789 and the "Terror" spanned the years 1792-94, by which time the young Peter Degraves had been living in England for at least nine or ten years. Indeed there is abundant evidence that his father began his medical practice in London no later than the beginning of 1780.[12] The strongest of this evidence is the fact that Parish records from the Church of St George the Martyr in Soho show that Peter Degraves was baptised there on 17 December 1780 and that his brother Henry was also baptised in the same church on the 18 September 1782 and that his parents were Peter and Ann Degravers.[13]

Peter Degraves' father is variously described as being an eminent, respected or wealthy doctor, though Degraves stated in his 1810 trial for burglary that he "lost his father in infancy and was brought up by his mother and his aunt".[14] However, this "loss" of his father was very different from the death that the term normally implies. "Loss" in this case covertly meant disappearance, though it is likely that the young Peter Degraves did wish his father had simply died—for the story of his

---

[12] *London Courant and Westminster Chronicle* 11th July 1780

[13] Register of Baptisms, Parish St George the Martyr (London) 1780 p. 167

[14] Taken from Peter Degraves' written defence to the charge of felony in the Lancaster Assizes in 1810, part of a bundle of court documents relating to the case held at the British National Archives: Item details HO 47/45/3

flamboyant and notorious father, was certainly an inheritance that he would have been ashamed to be connected with.

Peter Degraves' father was indeed a French doctor who was originally named Pierre De Gravers who joined the two components of his French surname to make "Degravers" and anglicised his Christian name to Peter. For the sake of clarity, and to eliminate confusion between father and son, the father will be referred to as Dr. Degravers and his son as Degraves where there is mention of the two persons in close proximity. Although Morris implied that Dr. Degravers and his family fled the "Terror", it is more likely that he left France for England to further his medical career in the late 1770s, long before the Terror became a serious issue for French citizens. Whilst the only published details about the life of Degravers come from a small biographical insert which was included in the 1992 reprint of his 1786 self-published book *A Complete Physico-Medical and Chirurgical Treatise on the Human Eye* we do know that as early as 1774 Dr Degravers was practicing as an eye surgeon in France and had already published, in French, his book on the human eye, copies of which are prominently displayed in his portrait.

In the English version of his book the author described himself as Dr. Peter Degravers, M.D. Professor of Anatomy and Physiology, the world authority on diseases of the eye. The book was probably published three times; firstly in France in 1774, in London in 1780 and, finally, in an extended form and with additional illustrations, in Edinburgh in 1786. The original editions of his book did not contain a biography, though their text is full of little anecdotes by the author highlighting the author's medical skills. The biography found in the reprinted version (part of a series called *The Classics of Ophthalmology Library* published by Gryphon) was put together by the publisher as an introduction to the work of Degravers, but sheds no light on the doctor's life prior to his arrival in England. It does admit, though, that he was largely unknown and had been regarded as a quack by most 19th century doctors. Certainly it seems that the treatment of eye diseases was an area of medicine that attracted quacks, there being many who were willing to part with a lot of money in the hope of restoring their sight.[15]

Due to the fact that Dr Degravers loved to place a portrait of himself in the front-piece of his books and because he was also a compulsive self-promoter it made finding out the truth about this complex character easier than is usual for persons from the 18th century. Also, as he frequently used the newspapers and other periodicals to keep himself and his medical practice in the public eye, there now exists in the recently digitalised, historic London and Edinburgh press a body of material that is sufficient to give a fascinating insight into Peter Degravers' enigmatic father's life after his arrival in England. It was a life that took many a twist and turn and which was never far from outrageous scandal.

In the foreword of each English edition of his book, Degravers politely draws the reader's attention to his linguistic skill by pointing out the fact that he was exclusively responsible for translating his treatise from French to English. The first English edition, published in 1780, was a fairly simple instructional textbook on treating diseases of the eye and contained a few basic drawings of cross-sections of the eye. The 1786 edition was a particularly lavish production with high-quality engravings with an additional section added concerning diseases of the ear. This later edition was almost certainly paid for by the doctor's short lived second wife, Elizabeth Baikie, and included an etched portrait of Dr. Degravers done by the famous Scottish barber, etcher and portrait artist John Kay, shown at the beginning of this chapter.[16]

---

[15] 'anon.' 'Quackery in Relation to Eye Diseases' *The British Medical Journal*
[16] *'anon.' The Oxford Journal* 1869, p.312

While details are sketchy, it can be reasonably assumed that Dr Degravers married Peter Degraves' English mother, Anne Jones, in the late 1770s. Anne Jones lived in Dover and was the daughter of a well-to-do family who made their fortune from an extensive transportation business, which included passenger coaches from Dover to various parts on inland England. Anne Jones had a sister Deborah (who also married a Frenchman) and a brother Charles. As Dover was the main gateway between France and England in the 18th century it is not surprising that both sisters married men from France.

The marriage of Dr Degravers and Anne Jones produced at least two children: Peter, probably in 1778, and his younger brother Henry, in the July 1782.[17] During the early 1780s records from a wide variety of London newspapers show that Dr Degravers operated a medical practice, specialising in eye surgery, in London out of his residence at Red Lion Square in Soho, where he and his young family lived.

Whilst Dr Degravers' practice also included general consultations his special interest was in diseases of the human eye. Degravers' particular and primary claim to fame and source of income appears to be that he performed the (at that time) very rare and difficult operation of removing cataracts from the eyes of his patients using a clever little surgical knife called a "kystitome". This was a surgical instrument with a fine double edged blade that was normally retracted inside of a thin sheath. The blade could be made to protrude at right angles to the sheath by pressing a button. The kystitome was Dr Degravers' tool of trade and in his book he described exactly how it was used

---

[17] Peter Degraves claimed his birthday to be 24 December 1778 however the parish baptism records of the church of St John the Martyr show him being born in Soho in November 1780. Why Degraves would want to fake his birth date is unclear. The same parish records show his brother Henry's birth date accurately as they correspond with the dates held in the British Library *India Office Records* .

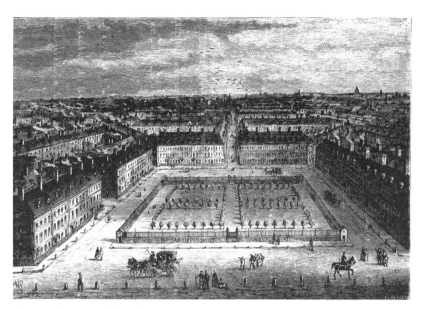

Figure 3 Red Lion Square, where Peter Degraves spent his early childhood, was a central meeting place for London's new intellectual elite in the late 18th century. Its coffee houses were popular with thinkers and innovators like Rennie, William Nicholson, James Watt, Joseph Priestly, Matthew Boulton (whose company made the Degraves shilling).

in an account that takes more than ten pages and reads somewhat like a handyman's guide to removing cataracts. Keeping in mind that Degravers was assuming that the "operator" following his written instructions had not performed the procedure previously, he advises that: "If the patient be of a good constitution…it will be unnecessary to prepare him for the operation by cooling drinks, bleeding or other indications…"

The operation, he stressed, should be performed on a sturdy table in a room darkened to dilate the patient's iris and that a strong assistant should stand behind the patient to hold his head immobile while the operation was undertaken (there was no local anaesthetic and the patient was fully conscious throughout the operation). While the patients head was being firmly held in the grip of a meaty assistant the doctor deftly slipped a speculum (a kind of eyeball-sized spoon) down between the eye socket and the rear of the eye to hold the eyelid off the eyeball and keep the whole eye still. With the patient's head firmly in hand and the eyeball in a wooden spoon Doctor Degravers advised that a very sharp knife be rested gently on the eye's membrane then inserted into the eye "with a slight pressure"; the operator taking great care not to cut the iris. Then the knife was to be carefully removed from the eye. At this point Dr Degravers suggested that the "operator" should explain to the (probably quite distraught) patient how important it was to keep his eye immobile "and that the pains he is about to suffer are not really as violent as he might imagine."

Once a cut in the eye had been made to the depth of the cataract the sheath of the kystitome was "introduced into the interior of the globe" of the eye via the fresh cut, the button was pushed to "have the blade out of its sheath" and cuts were made left and right and up and down around the cataract. If the patient was co-operating by holding his eye still and was not thrashing about on the table or screaming in agony the cataract was extracted by the operator "squeezing the globe of the eye softly" between his fingers until the cataract popped out of the eye via the passage created by the knives. Once the operation was complete Dr Degravers suggested a clean linen pad should be strapped over the eye and the patient bled by the arm regularly. But, the doctor advised, even after these regular bleedings there were still "numerous dangerous consequences" from complications that may await the patient "which might puzzle very much a young beginner" particularly as the idea of sterile surgical instruments and the use of antiseptics was not then part of medical practice. No doubt a significant number of the good doctor's patients succumbed to extremely painful, often fatal, infections of the eye after surgery.

How successful the doctor was at removing cataracts and how many of his patients were pleased with the results is not known; Dr Degravers, however, certainly promoted himself as the world's leading expert on treating diseases of the human eye in advertisements and "advertorials" in various newspapers and also through the sales of his book, which he advertised heavily in London newspapers from 1780 onwards. During the period from 1780 to 1784, as well as running his London practice, Degravers also gave a regular series of well-advertised lectures, complete with live surgical demonstrations. Thus, according to the *Morning Herald and Advertiser* of 10 February 1781:

> This Day Dr Degravers of the Red Lion Square will deliver the sixth lecture of his Physico-medical and Chirurgical course on the human eye. Such gentlemen students of the hospitals, who have obtained a ticket for the whole course are desired to take their seats as they come in on the right hand side of the theatre to prevent confusion as the preceding evenings. The subject of this lecture will consist in the accurate description of all the medical diseases incident to the human eye, together with the best method to cure them. The chair to be taken precisely at seven o'clock in the evening. The chirurgical disorders will come on the Saturday following.
>
> Terms of attendance are two guineas for which a Ticket is delivered at Dr Degravers' residence at Red-Lion Square ...

Such advertisements usually contained a mention of his book, which was offered for sale at the lectures. The two guineas entrance fee was a huge amount of money in the 1780s, representing about the same as a master mason's weekly wage or a month's wages for a labourer.[18] Thus the advertised lectures provided Degravers with a threefold income stream (with the ticket and book sales being supplemented by whatever actual medical work he gained through the increased awareness of his skills). This in itself was more important than it might at first seem as Degravers was able to exploit a loophole in the convention which prevented English medical practitioners from placing paid advertisements for their practices until the end of

---

[18] A. Gibson *Prices, food and Wages in Scotland 1550 to 1780* (London)

the 20th century.[19] For Degravers was not directly advertising his practice but his lectures and book. Without such a strategy, as a recent French émigré, he would have had to rely purely on word of mouth and social contacts to build up his medical practice, and associated income, in London.

Apart from being the world expert on diseases of the eye Doctor Degravers was also and expert and creative pioneer of dubious forms of newspaper advertising and direct sales techniques. This interesting accomplishment of the Doctor's is acknowledged by Hamish Mathison who, in his 1998 paper "Tropes of Well Being: Advertisement and the 18th Century Scottish Periodic Press". Mathison cites Degravers' later advertising campaigns in the Edinburgh newspapers as one of the earliest examples of deceptive advertising in British newspapers. For example in the *Caledonian Times* of 11 November 1786, Degravers placed what was supposedly an "open letter" from six of his former patients extensively praising his work and skills. Mathison maintains that the letter was a fake and was specifically designed to blur the lines between a genuine factual article and an advertisement.

Degravers began using this form of advertising at least as early as 1780 and continued to refine it through the 1780s in both London and Edinburgh. Indeed, he may well have been the pioneer of the now relatively common ploy of supporting a paid advertisement with a fictitious "testimonial" letter or a supposed news article. An example of a news article which appeared on the same page as his advertisements is shown below. This 'news article' was strategically placed on the same page as an advertisement for his lectures in the *Whitehall Evening Post* on 18 May 1784. Exactly the same news article, with an accompanying advertisement, appeared a week later in the *London Morning Herald and Daily Advertiser* on 28 May 1784.

---

[19] S. Lock *The Oxford Illustrated Companion to Medicine* (Oxford) 2001

> **Medical News:** We are informed Dr Degravers has attended the lovely Miss Sh----y and cured the complaint in her eyes which has baffled the attempts of several medical gentlemen...

The "news" piece then went on to promote Degravers' book and lectures. This suggests that the doctor possessed a shrewd business mind and that he used whatever means he could to promote himself, his lectures, his books and his reputation, none of which might ever have gained any attention from his peers or the public had it not been for the self-promotion campaign he sustained for most of the 1780s.

Another interesting insight into Degravers' approach to his lectures is that the notices for his lectures and the accompanying "news" pieces were most often placed on the newspapers' "Entertainment" page, alongside reports of stage performances and other diversions. Perhaps Degravers knew that there was an implicit offer of entertainment of an unusual kind in his promise in the *Morning Chronicle and London Advertiser* of 28 July 1781:

> A great many patients shall be dressed and operated upon in the lecture room... By such practical demonstrations those who attend this course shall undoubtedly acquire in very short time... practice of the most delicate part of the physic and surgery that would cost many years of study without such an opportunity.

Another "news" article, also on the entertainment page of the *Morning Chronicle and London Advertiser* of 19 February 1783, offered not only the chance to watch a live performance of Degravers removing cataracts from the eyes of conscious patients held down by a pair of muscular 'nurses', but also the opportunity to witness an event of almost Biblical proportions. Doctor Degravers promised to restore the sight of a 14-year-old boy who had been born blind. It can only be assumed that the operation was not a success as there was no mention of the promised miracle in London's newspapers over the following days. We can only speculate as to the boy's fate and how Degravers came by this unfortunate guinea pig in the first place. Who was this boy, possibly some blind street urchin Degravers had found begging on the streets of London and lured to the operating table with lavish promises? Indeed one must wonder from whence Degravers acquired the flow of patients for his live performances; whilst it would be fair to state that his procedural format certainly placed another connotation on the term "operating theatre".

Regardless of the success or popularity of these interesting public performances, Degravers' lectures and medical practice in London continued until the end of 1784. Then in November that year, he launched an advertising blitz, running at least six advertisements in various London newspapers that month. These ads were for a series of three lectures aimed specifically at surgeons from the army and navy. The first advertisement appeared in the *St James Chronicle* on 18 November in the format of an open letter, which began;

> "To His Majesties Navy and Army Surgeons. Gentlemen: Next week I will deliver the first of three lectures on the human eye …"

The advertisement went on to describe the benefits of attendance before concluding with a plug for his book. Yet, there is no evidence that this final lecture series ever took place for it was at this time that Dr Degravers suddenly disappeared from the London scene.

It is not known exactly why Degravers decamped from London, where both his family and medical practice were located, though it may have had something to do with this last lecture series.

Perhaps something went terribly wrong during one of his surgical demonstrations? Or perhaps it was something as simple as issues of debt?

When Degravers reappeared in the Scottish capital, Edinburgh, in late 1786 he began advertising a fresh round of lectures as well as his medical practice. Either economic conditions, or his expectations, had changed significantly, however, for now he charged a single, simple fee of half a crown per consultation— whilst the cost of attending his lectures had dropped from two guineas to one shilling. As there were 22 shillings in a guinea this was a considerable devaluation of the entrance fee, which might have reflected a less affluent potential audience or an attempt to get higher attendance figures in a smaller market with an emphasis on making the public aware of his arrival in Edinburgh.

It is regularly mentioned in third-party references to Dr Degravers that he was a man with a high opinion of himself who was generally able to convince others of the worth of his self-evaluation. There were many, however, who regarded him as a quack—a label that some of his wilder publicity-seeking antics would have done little to dispel. Perhaps the best example of this was when he became associated with the famous case of the convicted Edinburgh criminal Deacon William Brodie, on whose character and actions Robert Louise Stevenson is said to have based his novel *Doctor Jekyll and Mister Hyde*.[20] William Brodie was the son of a well respected and affluent businessman in Edinburgh who was also a member of the Edinburgh Town Council. On his father's death William Brodie moved into his father's position on the City Council and was also appointed Deacon of the incorporated body of Wrights and Masons in Edinburgh. Occupying these two socially elevated positions (and with the wealth he inherited from his father) the charming

---

[20] E. Simpson *The Robert Louis Stevenson Originals* (London) 2005

Deacon William Brodie moved freely about the city and was welcome in the homes of the members of Edinburgh's social and financial elite. He also attended all those social events that were part of the rounds in the highest levels of Society. However the fact was that for most of his adult life Deacon Brodie had led a double life. He had a dark and secret side which he kept well hidden from polite society, for when he was not mixing with Edinburgh's gentry Brodie was mixing with its low life. Deacon Brodie had a clutch of "degrading" vices most of which he was able to satisfy by regular visits to "...a house of the most disreputable description kept by a Mr Clarke in the Fleshmarket Close." Brodie's various vices included gambling and it was the debts accumulated from that sport and the need to be able to finance his passions in the brothels at Fleshmarket Close that led Brodie to "... league himself with desperate men...of the lowest grade and most abandoned principles.

Brodie gathered around himself a gang of criminals with whom he began a campaign of brazen burglaries and robberies. Using his intimate knowledge of the homes and business premises of Edinburgh's wealthy population Brodie began to rob his friends and associates. So audacious, unrelenting and thorough were these robberies that all of Edinburgh was profoundly alarmed. An example of just how audacious Brodie became, and how sure he was that no-one would ever guess his true identity, is provided by the description of a robbery he committed one Sunday morning on one of his circle of friends, a wealthy widow. This woman was usually to be found at Church every Sunday, but on this particular day she was feeling unwell and did not attend. Sitting in her home she was surprised when a masked man walked into the room in which she sat and, whilst

KAY DEL SULP 1788

Mr. BRODIE

Figure 4: Deacon William Brodie, who Dr Degravers promised to resurrect from the dead after his execution, was used by Robert Louise Stevenson as the model for the main character in his famous novel *Doctor Jekyll and Mister Hyde.*

21

brandishing a pistol, calmly walked past her straight to her bureau and opened the top drawer, which was where she kept a considerable sum of cash. He removed the money, bowed briefly to his dumbfounded victim, and was gone with neither party having spoken a single word.

Brodie's crime spree went on for a number of years until he was eventually caught and sentenced to death by hanging. All witnesses present in court were extremely impressed by how calmly Deacon Brodie took the "guilty" verdict and the sentence of death. Even as he mounted the steps of the scaffold where the noose awaited his neck he chatted calmly with those of his friends who had come to witness his hanging. What the gathered public did not know was that Deacon Brodie had done a deal with Doctor Degravers.

It is a comment on Dr Degravers' salesmanship that he had convinced the condemned Brodie that his medical talents were such that he would be able to bring him back to life after he had been executed and, on this basis, the Doctor was paid a considerable sum (in advance) by Brodie before the day of execution.[21] Dr Degravers accompanied Brodie to the gallows and immediately after the execution Brodie's body was taken down from the scaffold, put in a waiting cart and rushed to Dr Degravers' surgery where the doctor lanced the dead man's temples and arms at points which he had marked on Brodie immediately before the execution. As with the blind boy the good Doctor's opinion of his skills exceeded his actual ability and his attempted resurrection of the dead Deacon was unsuccessful.

However, despite this failure, Degravers' Edinburgh medical practice (backed up by his undoubted skills of self-promotion and misleading advertising) was doing well enough for him to

---

[21] J. Gibson *Deacon Brodie Father to Jekyll and Hyde* (Edinburgh) 1993

both move up in society and to also obtain sufficient credit from the various businesses in town to enable him to live in the manner to which he was accustomed. On the circuit of parties around Edinburgh's society Dr Degravers met the young Elisabeth Baikie, the daughter of a propertied well-to-do Orkney family and sister of Robert Baikie M.P., the Seventh Earl of Tankerness. Apart from her family's wealth Miss Baikie owned her own pleasant, fully furnished home in Edinburgh and came with a £700 dowry. The charming, mature and indebted French doctor wooed and soon wed the young Miss Baikie. They were married in Edinburgh's Roman Catholic Cathedral at Midlothian, on 29 April 1787 less than a year after Degravers' arrival in Scotland. Sadly their union did not last long for less than a year later, despite the doctor's professed skills, the new Mrs Degravers "died on child bed" while giving birth to a daughter, Eliza. By this time the family and friends of the deceased young woman had begun to become aware of whispers and rumours concerning Dr Degravers, whose dubious character and rapidly accumulating debts around town had become well known. These well-wishers   ensured that Elisabeth's home and money went not towards covering the Doctor's debts and flamboyant lifestyle but directly to the couple's new daughter.[22] Degravers plans to establish a new life in Scotland were foiled by this manoeuvre of his dead wife's relatives so he responded by abandoning his daughter and fleeing Edinburgh, leaving his now considerable new debts and once more disappeared from view for several years.

An interesting side note to all this, which helps us understand Peter Degraves' relationship with his father, is that Doctor Degravers and Elisabeth Baikie were both Roman Catholics

---

[22] A consequence of Doctor Degraves' two years in Edinburgh was that his son Peter now had a half sister, Eliza Degravers. Eliza went on to marry Captain Malcolm Cowan of the Royal Navy; their grandson William became the 9th Earl of Tankerness after his uncle, Eliza's nephew, died without issue.

(they were married in the Roman Catholic cathedral in Edinburgh); so it seems extremely unlikely that he had divorced his previous wife Anne, the mother of his sons Peter and Henry. Even for non-Roman Catholics a divorce was almost impossible to obtain in the late eighteenth century. As we know that the first Mrs Degravers did not die until at least after the end of 1821, it is certain that the doctor's marriage to Elisabeth Baikie was both dishonourable and bigamous.[23]

As a result of his actions in both Edinburgh and London Dr Degravers would have found it almost impossible to practise medicine in any city in the British Isles. Finding his options limited Degravers did as many other desperate men of that time did and took to the sea. The next phase of the Doctor's colourful life is preserved in letters he wrote in 1790 to the owner of the British slave-trading company James Rogers & Co. From these it is clear that, sometime after fleeing Edinburgh, Pierre Degravers gained employment as the medical officer on board a slave ship called the *Pearl*, owned by the aforesaid Bath-based slave-trading company. In a letter to his employer, James Rogers, Degravers shows himself to be a strong supporter of the slave trade.

> I have now finished (writing) the *History of the Kingdom of Haifock*, commonly called Old Calabar... I have not mentioned the transactions of your ship masters, nor those of others, leading to the ideas which a copy of my journal have naturally raised within you; the barbarians would most undoubtedly have been productive of another argument to abolish the slave trade, which obviously is clearly demonstrated humane in the actual state of that part of Africa. [24]

---

[23] Bonwick Transcripts, *Letter from Degraves to Bathurst* 18th Dec. 1822
[24] PRO, Chancery Masters Exhibits C/107/7 *P Degravers to James Rogers.*

There is no evidence that the doctor's *History of the Kingdom of Haifock* was ever published and, unfortunately, neither the manuscript nor his journal can be located.

It is likely that Dr Degravers entered employment with Rogers and Co. almost immediately after fleeing Edinburgh, probably in early 1788 when the British Parliament enacted *Dolben's Act*, which made it a legal requirement that all British slave ships carry a surgeon on board. *Dolben's Act* was an attempt by Parliament to reduce the mortality rate of slaves and crew aboard ships carrying slaves from the African coast to the various ports of the British Empire, particularly the West Indies. For Degravers the timing of the Act was fortuitous as it created both a demand for surgeons and favourable salary conditions. Under the provisions of the Act doctors were not only paid a base wage, but also a bonus based on the rate of mortality on board their ship. This amounted to around one shilling per slave that made it to the slave market in good health and a further incentive of £50 if the mortality rate for a voyage was kept below two percent.[25] As well as these monetary incentives, the ship's surgeon was usually entitled to an additional bonus of two slaves at the end of the journey, one male and one female. Despite the pay, however, the life of a slave ship's surgeon could not be considered an easy one. Degravers would have had to live on board in squalid, fetid conditions for months and would have spent a considerable amount of time every day below decks in the stench and misery of the slave quarters. In these conditions he was expected to treat a wide range of illness, from dysentery and diarrhoea to syphilis and typhoid as well as the injuries from whippings, friction sores, rat bites and other infected wounds. An insight into conditions on board the slave ship *Pearl* comes from another letter written by Dr Degravers to his employer.

---

[25] R. Sheridan 'The Guinea Surgeons of the Middle Passage' *International Journal of African Historical Studies* Vol. 14, No. 4 (1981)

Here, I am sorry to inform you, we have lost 113 slaves, but when I consider that many were bought against my opinion & others without my advice, I do not wonder at such a loss... this last misfortune is owing to a total contempt of the laws of Parliament & the articles. All the white people are and have been starved; as to the blacks, their loss is owing to a purchase of bad yams which never fail to give the flux to all those that eat them. Our bread is all mouldy and I am much afraid of the consequences, in short, Sir, it appears evident to me that you have depended on people who are incapable to carry on a trade so extensive, perplexing, and dubious. I could tell you more, but they should be descriptions of such cruelty, that I would not commit to paper.

Indeed it was the combination of the terrible working conditions and the excellent remuneration that attracted only a specific type of medical man to this job, leading a social commentator of the time, Doctor Falconbridge, to note that:

"...surgeons employed in the Guinea trade are generally driven to engage in so disagreeable an employ by the confined state of their finances."[26]

As well as being responsible for the health of the slaves and the crew, slave ship surgeons were also required to keep a detailed log of the illnesses and causes of death of all persons aboard their ship.

While the combination of an attractive salary and a convenient means to escape his creditors in Edinburgh goes a long way to explaining Degravers' decision to take up this occupation, his change of circumstance occasioned another considerable drop in professional and social standing. Nevertheless, it was certainly better than having to endure the shame of debtors' prison. Indeed, Degravers (like his son Peter) seems always to have tried to make the best of whatever situation he found himself in, regardless of the cost to others.

---

[26] A. Falconbridge *An Account of the Slave Trade on the Coast of Africa*

Degravers' first trip on the slave ship *Pearl* was to pick up a cargo of slaves from the infamous slave port of Calabar in what is now the south east corner of Nigeria. In the days of Dr Degravers Calabar was a small kingdom with an economy based on the supplying slaves to the British for use in the West Indies. The majority of slaves traded were captured from the neighbouring country of Igbo and were particularly sought after by plantation owners because the Igbo were from an agriculturally based society and so worked well on the plantations. This first voyage, referred to in the letter above, did not afford Degravers a performance bonus because the mortality rate for the slaves was well above the "less than 2%" that would have given him his extra money and two slaves. Incredibly the *Pearl's* death rate was above 25%, even before they left port! Of course Dr Degravers tried to blame the captain of the *Pearl* for the high mortality levels whilst the captain of the *Pearl*, William Blake, blamed Dr Degravers:

> … I believe we have been very sickly and Buried 131 men 45 woman Slaves and still Burying. I am sorry to say Wilding is Dead and several more (of the crew), our Ship now is very short of hands which is mostly the case with the other Ships – M[r] Stribling Must go Master of the Ship, to keep the *Pearl* here would ruin every thing as we are burying of slaves and Buryed so many – our Doctor is short of the judgment he pretended to have; he is not suitable to Slaves,

So it seems, once again, that Dr Degravers' opinion of his abilities was not borne out by statistical reality however he did not let the high death rate of the slaves interfere with his scholarly pursuits for in his spare time aboard the *Pearl* when not writing his book on the history of the Kingdom of Haifock, Dr Degravers turned his attention to the long standing problem of accurately calculating Longitude.

Figure 5: Dr Degravers, now a slave ship surgeon, spent most of his working day below the deck amongst filth and the suffering of slaves, four of whom he could claim as a bonus if he kept the death rate low enough.

In pursuit of this scholarly task it is likely the Doctor was motivated not only by love of science but also by the substantial rewards (between £10,000 and £20,000) offered by the British Government's Longitude Board for the discovery of methods to improve navigational accuracy and safety. The primary objective of the Longitude Board was to stimulate the discovery of an accurate and reliable method for calculating longitude whilst at sea, but the Board also included rewards for other advancements in navigation and shipping.

Quitting his seafaring life in 1792 Degravers and a French colleague named Henry Ould worked on a revolutionary new method to determine Longitude and in 1794 submitted to the Board a paper called *"The Longitude discovered, by a new Mathematical Instrument, called Graphor."*

Unfortunately for the partnership of Degravers & Ould, contemporary developments in determining longitude with the chronometer and improvements to the sextant had largely satisfied the Board's requirements in this area and their paper was rejected. Despite this setback Degravers continued to promote the Graphor, and its associated "*New Mathematics*" maintaining that its astounding advantages had not been fully appreciated by the conservative minds of the Longitude Board. To help his cause he resorted to his familiar tactics of employing the London press to promote his invention. He and Ould published an open letter to the Board of Longitude in several London newspapers and journals. In this letter they explained the basics of the "*New Mathematics*" in order to try to pressure the Board to reconsider the rejection of their invention. Sadly for the two inventors, not only was the Board not moved, but the tactic resulted in several unfavourable reviews of the Graphor and the associated New Mathematics, such as the one below by Hookham and Carpenter in the *Monthly Catalogue*.

> "*The Longitude discovered, by a new Mathematical Instrument, called Graphor.*"
> We have heard so often of the Longitude being discovered that, on reading the title of this Book, we were very willing to make allowances for the author's sanguine expectations, and to be reconciled to the event, if it should be found that this grand geographical mystery had eluded his most accurate researches. With this resignation we opened the work; but notwithstanding the positive assurances of the writer, that the secret was discovered, our natural incredulity took possession of us, when we found that the Board of Longitude had been applied to, but had not designed to take notice of the communication..." [27]

Degravers' response to these rejections was to offer his system up for public scrutiny by appointment at his residence. Indeed,

---

[27] Hookham and Carpenter *The Critical Review* Ed. T. Smollett (London)

he went further, advertising an opportunity for the public to invest by subscription in his invention through an interesting instrument involving an "independent" trustee. Hookham and Carpenter described the device in *The Critical Review*:

> "Before the public is favoured with a description of this wonderful instrument (the Graphor), a subscription is requested, which, when it amounts to £20,000 is to be, at the discretion of twelve able persons chosen by the subscribers, who are to examine the merits of the instrument, and if it answers, the inventors are to call upon the subscribers for the money. In the mean time, any person wishing to have a sight of the instrument, is desired to send a letter, post paid, to Messrs. Peter Degravers, M.D. and Henry Ould, at the Literary Assembly, No. 15. Old Bond Street; and a few days after they will receive a letter with an appointment to see it."

Unfortunately for Degravers and Ould, the public perception of the inventor's claims for the Graphor's commercial potential appears to have been affected by the negative reviews and the ambitious target of £20,000 in subscriptions was never reached. The result of these public rebuffs was that the Graphor, the "New Mathematics" and Degravers disappeared from London altogether and the 1794 attempt to claim a financial reward from the Longitude Board and the subsequent media coverage appears to have been the last time that the flamboyant doctor attempted to employ the press in an exercise of self-promotion. Indeed, at this point in time it appears that Dr Degravers entirely disappeared from history.

Chapter Three: Businessman, Bankrupt and Burglar

During the period when Dr Degravers was executing his various schemes, plans and exploits it is not clear exactly what his eldest son, Peter, was doing other than that he was not with his father. As there is general agreement that Peter Degraves was born in 1778, he would have been about 6 or 7 years old when his father fled London. We also know that in later life Degraves would say that this was when his father died.[28] While we do not know the details, it can be reasonably assumed, based on his later accomplishments, that through the 1780's and early 1790's Peter Degraves must have been attending a good school in England and that he had yet to drop the offending 'r' from his surname.

Likewise we do not know exactly how Dr Degravers' first wife, Mrs Anne Degravers, supported her young family other than that she moved in with her wealthy, widowed sister Deborah Decharme, who had also married a Frenchman.

Deborah Jones married a wealthy French merchant named Jean Decharme, who kept a house in London as well as one in his home town of Caen in France. Jean Decharme, who died in 1788 without children, left his considerable fortune to his wife.

In this situation the young Peter Degraves would have been like a son to his childless, but very wealthy, Aunt; a relationship that he would later exploit to gain financial support from her for his various ventures. Sadly Decharme's support for her nephew's grand designs ultimately resulted in the loss of her fortune and

---

[28] On page four of Peter Degraves' written defence, which was read to the jury in his 1810 felony trial, he states that "... I am the son of a Physician in Town, whose loss I have had to lament from infancy..."

31

her commitment to an asylum for the insane. It is also likely that Degraves' mother turned to her parents who, the evidence suggests, were wealthy.

Apart from these meagre details we know very little of Peter Degraves' early family life other than that he had at least one sibling, his younger brother Henry, who had probably been named by Dr Degravers after his friend and co-inventor of the Graphor, Henry Ould. [29] It is the young Henry Degraves/Degravers' military records that confirm, without doubt, that Dr Pierre De Gravers/Degravers was the father of Peter and Henry. When Henry enlisted as a cadet in 1799 his surname was spelt Degravers, but sometime after he began service in India the spelling was changed to Degraves.[30] The same military records show that Henry's father's name was Peter Degravers. We do not know the exact reason for the family's decision to change the spelling of their name, but it would be reasonable to assume that Mrs Degravers had eventually been made aware of the bigamous and debt-ridden status of her husband in Edinburgh. The existence of such a scandal would have made some disassociation from him a social necessity.

At this point a brief look at the life of Henry Degraves is important in developing an understanding of the various relationships which would become pivotal in the life of his brother; for while Peter Degraves followed his ambitions along an entrepreneurial path into trade and industry, his brother Henry chose the more secure path of the military. After completing his studies as a cadet in 1799, Henry joined the East

---

[29] Peter Degraves later named his eldest son after his brother Henry, breaking the family tradition common in the 18th and 19th centuries of naming the eldest son after the father.

[30] *British Library Collections, India office;* Degravers, Henry

32

India Company Army in Madras.[31] By the end of the 18th century a commission in the Indian Army had become valuable due to the access it gave officers to trade opportunities as well as unofficial tax receipts from local businesses. For this reason it not only required a personal nomination from one of the East India Company's Court of Directors but also cost a significant sum of money. That Henry Degraves was able to meet both of these requirements suggests that he and his brother had influential or wealthy patrons, probably their mother's parents.[32]

As a career soldier Henry Degraves spent most of his life in India around the area of Madras, progressing up through the ranks to eventually become a Lieutenant Colonel. In Madras Henry Degraves joined the 8th Regiment of Native Infantry as a second lieutenant and served under the direct command of Captain Hugh Macintosh. In 1803 he fought in the Marathas Wars and was involved in the "White Mutiny" of 1809 when the officers of the East India Company's Army commanding the Native Infantry in Madras rebelled against the rule of the newly appointed Governor, Sir George Barlow. At the time of the White Mutiny Hugh Macintosh was in command of the 1st battalion of the 8th Regiment of Native Infantry and Henry Degraves was one of his Lieutenants.[33] The interesting and close relationship between Henry Degraves and Captain Macintosh will be dealt with in greater detail in the chapter concerning Macintosh. Henry Degraves predeceased his brother, Peter, by almost 20 years, dying in Wallajahbad near Madras in 1834 at the age of 52.

Peter Degraves is always said to have grown up in Dover, however, no records can be found to confirm this. It is more likely that he spent his first years at Red Lion Square in Soho in

---

[31] *The India Office and Burma Office List* (Bombay) 1824 p.218
[32] A. Cardew *The White Mutiny* (Bombay) 1926 p.3
[33] *Oriental Herald* 1827, p. 202

his father's home and that he later moved to Dover to live with this Aunt or grandparents. Degraves describes his education as having been "liberal". While in the late 18th century a "classical" education implied one that placed paramount importance on fluency in Greek, Latin and the classics, a "liberal" education was defined as that:

> "...which makes a man an intellectual freeman, as opposed to that which makes a man a tool, an instrument for the accomplishment of some aim or object. The aim of the liberal education ... is the right use of the realised capital of extant knowledge..."[34]

Because Degraves, in his sworn statement to the jury in his 1810 trial, said that he went straight into an apprenticeship with a mercantile business at the completion of his school years it can reasonably be claimed that, later, contradictory, reports concerning the activities and studies he undertook in his early life are false. Interestingly most of these reports emanated from Degraves himself.

These reports are found in the various existing histories of Degraves' life. One reoccurring claim is that Degraves studied law, and according to Hooper "he spent about two years studying at Gray's Inn, one of the three Inns of Court seated in London". These claims all appear to be based around letters Degraves wrote to Governor Arthur from Hobart goal between 1826 and 1832. Degraves also claimed that he worked for the famous English physicist William Nicholson, who had been his father's neighbour in Red Lion Square. As he put it:

> I was for several years principal assistant to the late Mr Nicholson Esq, formerly secretary to the Chamber of Arts, editor of the Philosophical Journal, and many other scientific

---

[34] W. Atkinson *Liberal Education of the 19th Century*, (New York) 1878

works, engineer to almost all the water works in London, and the vicinity, and also those at Gosport and Portsmouth and many other engineering undertakings, and previous to the experience which Mr Nicholson's office, laboratory and factory afforded me.

These claims serve well to illustrate Degraves' propensity for self-promotion and exaggeration. For the facts are that in all the writings about the life and activities of William Nicholson (1753–1815), including a biography written by Nicholson's eldest son held in Oxford's Bodleian Library, there is no mention of Peter Degraves in any form and certainly not as Nicholson's principal assistant. Also Nicholson had no factory, was not responsible for "almost all the water works in London" and was only an occasional consultant for the water works at Gosport and Portsmouth, which position he quit in 1810 before the completion of the works.[35] It is interesting that Degraves exaggerated William Nicholson's achievements in order to boost his own claimed levels of expertise. In fact, for the five years up until to his death in 1815 Nicholson was in poor health and in a state of financial "embarrassment".

Hooper, Allport and Bingham also all state that Degraves studied engineering under the famous Scottish civil engineer John Rennie. From 1791 on Rennie did indeed operate an engineering business at Blackfriars in London where, for about a decade, he specialised in building canals then bridges and docks. Interestingly Rennie mixed in the same circles as William Nicholson, circles which included James Watt and Matthew Boulton. Further insight into how Degraves constructed his fictional past is given by the fact that Rennie, Nicholson and Boulton's residences, and Gray's Inn, were all located within a short distance of Red Lion Square, where Degraves grew up, so it is likely that Degraves was familiar enough with each entity to

---

[35] ' Memoir of the Late Mr. W. Nicholson' *The Gentleman's Magazine*

either fabricate or exaggerate a relationship with them. For while it is possible that, for example, the young Degraves and Rennie may have met, there are problems with the conventional accounts which imply a long and intimate relationship. In the 18th century to 'study' under an engineer such as Rennie implied an apprenticeship, of which the standard term was seven years. Indeed Giblin, in his book *The Early History of Tasmania*, specifically states that Degraves served an apprenticeship with John Rennie and had actually developed a practice in civil engineering prior to deciding to take his family to Hobart. However in his trial in the Assizes in 1810 Degraves swears that he was apprenticed to the London mercantile house of Railton and Ranking until at least the end of the 1790s. Once he left Railton and Ranking we know that he ran several small businesses in and around Manchester and London from about 1803 until 1810, so it is difficult to imagine how he could have managed to study under Rennie and Nicholson and also study law at the Inns of Court in that same period of time.[36] Yet Degraves' obituary in the *Hobart Courier* states that Degraves was *"with Rennie in his early life"*, which can certainly be taken to mean that he studied with Rennie no later than in his mid twenties. Despite the obvious problems with timing, Bingham, Hooper, Giblin and Allport all contend that Peter Degraves also studied architecture and mathematics. Further, *The Companion to Tasmanian History* states that he was an engineer who also studied Law and Architecture, while Allport adds that Degraves was a highly competent surveyor and also "an authority on boring for water" and that he supervised important water boring projects when he carried out work for both the Duchess of Buccleuch and the Marquis of Stafford in the County of Surrey. Degraves also mentions these supposed water works in his letters.

---

[36] Degraves' written defence read to jury Lancaster Assizes 1810

There are very strong reasons to doubt that Degraves supervised, or even took part in, these works.[37] Thomas Allen's book *A History of the County of Surrey* published in 1831 describes both these events in detail. It states that the work was "done under the direction of Mr. Selfe from Kingston, assisted by Whiteland, from Richmond." There is no mention of Degraves' involvement on any level, this despite the fact that Degraves (from Hobart prison) supplied the *Colonial Times* with the following details:

> In the Duchess of Buccleuch's garden, at Richmond, Mr. Degraves superintended the sinking of boring rods to the depth of 364 feet when the finest rock water imaginable began to issue 56 feet above the ground… The Marquis of Stafford was in consequence induced to try a similar experiment, which Mr Degraves superintended with equal success; for, after having bored to a depth of 352 feet water rose 51 feet above the surface, affording a constant supply of water to his Lordship's premises.

However, Allen's *History of Surrey* states that the Marquis' bore was the first one dug, that the water rose 15 feet above the surface and that a small engine, erected by a Mr. Euston, pumped the water a further "110 feet perpendicular at a distance of 140 yards from the engine to the house, having a reservoir on the top, which is always supplied." The Duchess of Buccleuch's bore, being of lower elevation and closer to the river was only 254 feet deep and the water rose 26 feet above the surface.[38]

It is possible that Degraves either witnessed or heard of these two projects, but there is no evidence at all of his involvement as a supervisor or on any other level. At best, as with his claims to have studied with so many famous people, Degraves' appears to have manipulated the truth, exaggerating the importance of his

---

[38] T. Allen *A History of the County of Surrey* (London) 1831 pp. 432-433

involvement, by exploiting the poor communication systems of the time to his own advantage (a skill he may have learned from his father). The most likely reason for this particular piece of self-promotion was that he hoped that his claim of having worked for members of the nobility would give a considerable boost to his social and professional status in the young Colony. He may also have hoped that it might increase his chances of an early release from the Hobart goal where, at the time he wrote the letter, he had spent almost one year.

In stark contrast to the mythology which has grown around Degraves the archival material, from the Manchester Trade Directory of 1804, reveals the true and diminutive nature of his supposedly vast business empire. In 1804 the Trade Directory states that he was operating as a manufacturer of muslin and other articles in Manchester. That he does not appear in Manchester Trade Directory of 1802 or in the subsequent 1806 directory indicates that this business was relatively short lived. Confirmation of this is provided by a notice that appeared in the *London Gazette* of 1805 in which Degraves advertised that:

> … the Partnership heretofore
> fulfilling between Peter Degraves, of Manchester, in
> the County of Lancaster, James Lane, of the City of London
> and George Dickinson, of Kirkby Steven, in the county of
> Westmoreland, Cotton-Manufacturers, was dissolved by
> Consent on the 25th Day of March last, so far as respects
> the said George Dickinson. All debts due to or owing by
> the said Concern will be received and paid by the said Peter
> Degraves and James Lane. As witness the Hands of the
> Parties the 16th day of April 1805,
> *Peter Degraves*
> *James Lane*
> George Dickinson

The new business of Degraves and Lane (less Dickinson) also did not last very long. In 1807 the *London Gazette* gave notice that, as the result of a hearing on 19 May 1807, the Commissioners of the Commission of Bankrupts had awarded against *"... Peter Degraves of Cheapside in the City of London and of Manchester... Warehouseman, Dealer, Chapman... carrying out business under the firm of Peter Degraves and Company".*[39] The result of this was that Degraves was declared bankrupt and his estate and effects were sold off to pay a dividend to his creditors. In the same year Degraves sued his business partner, James Lane. Two years later whilst still bankrupt, he also sued a Mr. McMullen.

Much can be learned about Degraves' method of conducting business by examining the cotton 'manufacturing' enterprise he set up in association with Lane and Dickinson. The premises at Kirkby Stephen were originally purchased by Dickinson in 1803 as a farmhouse with orchards and outbuildings. Sometime before 1807 the property was purchased by Peter Degraves and his business "partner", his auntie Deborah Decharme, with Dickinson becoming a "tenant" in the house. The ownership of the property was then transferred to the Company of Degraves, Lane and Dickinson & Co and during this period a factory building was constructed. It seems unlikely that the factory actually ever produced anything as the Company went into bankruptcy less than 12 months after the building was completed.[40]

The basis of the relationship between Degraves and his auntie, Deborah Decharme, is interesting as is the fact that in late 1809 Deborah Decharme, was the assignee of the bankrupt Degraves, indicating she was the principle creditor (that is to say Degraves owed his Aunt more money than he owed anyone else). As such

---

[39] *London Gazette*, 1807, pages 187, 653 and 800
[40] Braithwaite *A Guide-book to Kirkby Stephen,* (London) 1922

Decharme sued (unsuccessfully) Degraves' ex-partner James Lane over the proceeds of a promissory note that had been made out to Lane and Degraves jointly. That she did not sue Degraves indicates that while she was his principle creditor she was also his sympathetic financial backer.

Over the period between 1806 and 1810 there were at least six other separate court actions initiated by or against Degraves, though there may have been more that have not yet been uncovered. These were all civil matters except for a criminal case against Degraves, tried in the Lancaster Assizes, which occurred in 1810.

The court records from his 1810 Lancaster Assizes trial provide some illuminating insights into the workings of Peter Degraves' mind and how he dealt with difficulties. The trial records show that Degraves was convicted of larceny for stealing a large quantity of goods, mostly parcels of an expensive French fabric called cambric, valued at between £2,000 and £3,000 (an extremely large sum of money in 1810 that would convert to about $200,000 in today's money). The stolen goods belonged to a Mr John Parsons, a "friend" who had left Degraves' employ to start his own business as a merchant in Manchester some years previous. Degraves stole the goods from a warehouse owned by Thomas Bainbridge, also a person whom Degraves had considered a "friend" and who was also a former business partner. Degraves' conviction on this charge resulted in him being sentenced to 12 months in prison. It is a good indication of his social and family connections that, despite being convicted by a jury and subsequently serving one year in King's Gate prison, Peter Degraves was pardoned some time after his release in 1811.[41] It is also worth comparing Degraves' sentence with that of the less socially connected James Munro, a 20-year-old boatswain, who, in 1799, was found guilty in the Old Bailey of

---

[41] *UK National Archives* HO 47/45/3

stealing 20 yards of calico valued at £12 (about $800 in today's money) and sentenced to transportation to New South Wales for seven years or with Mary Reibey who, at 13 years old, was also sentenced to transportation to Australia for stealing a horse.

The witness statements from the Lancaster trial provide surprising detail of Degraves' crime and offer further insights into his personality and amoral mode of operating. The trial was held in Manchester at the end of March 1810. Earlier that month, Degraves had travelled to Lancashire from London (where he claims to have owned a very large business, though it was almost certainly owned by his aunt). His aim, apparently, was to visit his two friends Parsons (who had previously been employed as a head clerk by Degraves' in London) and Bainbridge, who owned a large warehouse in Manchester which Degraves occasionally used.[42] In one of the lockable rooms of that warehouse Parsons had stored a large quantity of French cambric, a very finely woven lightweight cotton fabric often used for lace and expensive handkerchiefs.

To back track a little we find that in late February 1810 Degraves' new head clerk, Mr Swan, had discovered an error in the accounts that favoured one of the firm's customers, a Mr Bland. Mr Bland had also been Degraves' partner in some business transactions and often acted as his agent. Degraves immediately assumed that the book keeping mistake was a deliberate conspiracy by Bland and Parsons to defraud him but, rather than confronting the two men and asking for an explanation, he decided to take matters into his own hands.

---

[42] Witnesses in this trial stated that Degraves was in business in a very large way in London but court documents from a bankruptcy trial that took place a few months earlier, on the 16th of December 1809, (Decharme and Waine Vs Lane) state that in December 1809 Peter Degraves was still bankrupt. It is therefore likely that the business Degraves was running in 1809 and 1810 was owned by a third "silent" party, probably his auntie Deborah Decharme.

Arriving in Manchester on the 10th March Degraves pretended to visit Bainbridge and Parsons for purely social reasons, having lunch and then dinner with them. The three men arranged to eat together again on the evening of Thursday the 15th March, but in the afternoon of that day Degraves pretended to be sick "from having drunk too much wine" the preceding evening and sent them a message asking to be excused from their dinner engagement.

In the meantime Degraves had somehow obtained a key to Parsons' storeroom at Bainbridge's warehouse and, late on Thursday evening, around 11 p.m., knowing Bainbridge and Parsons were then dining together, he entered the storeroom room and removed three or four large parcels of cambric. He transported the stolen goods in the back of a hired chaise to the Red Lion Hotel where he had already rented a room. There he repacked the fabric into trunks, which he then transported to the White Lion Hotel where he had rented another room for the purpose of hiding the stolen goods. The night's work complete Degraves returned to his room at the Red Lion for a well earned rest.

The following morning Degraves met Parsons for breakfast where an upset Parsons told him that all his cambric was gone. Degraves pretended he knew nothing of the night's events and went with Parsons to inspect the scene of the crime where he pointed out anchor marks drawn with white chalk around the room. These, Degraves ventured, might, perhaps, be excise marks and that it appeared that the excise officers had come in the night and seized Parsons' goods for outstanding duty. Then Degraves, feigning a desire to help Parsons, suggested he should speak to a lawyer to see what might be done; Degraves was even good enough to suggest a couple of lawyers he knew with expertise in excise law. Certain that his cunning plan had worked Degraves left Parsons for a few hours, but they met later that day, at about 2 p.m., when they dined with Bainbridge at the

Commercial Inn. There Parsons informed the others that he had "made enquiries and was pretty certain no seizure had been made by the Excise Office" and that the loss of his goods could only have been by robbery.

Degraves professed that he still considered it unlikely that the goods had been stolen and that there was probably still a good chance that excise officers had them. He then asked Bainbridge and Parsons for a loan of £10 for his coach fare back to London as he had run out of cash. Parsons lent him the money.

Now possessing not only Parsons' valuable French cambric but also with Parson's £10 note in his pocket a satisfied Degraves returned to the White Lion hotel in a hired chaise ready to return to London. Sadly for Degraves, when the horseman pulled the chaise up in front of the White Lion Degraves found two excise officers waiting for him for, as it turned out, the owners of the Red Lion and the White Lion knew each other well and had compared notes about the man who had rented rooms for himself in both their establishments. Deciding that there was something suspicious going on they informed the Excise Office that they suspected Degraves of smuggling. Taking Degraves upstairs to the room containing the stolen cambric the officer in charge demanded to see Degraves' excise receipts and Degraves, rather than admit he had stolen the fabrics, pretended he had actually smuggled the goods and tried to bribe the excise officers by offering them £30 in cash to turn a blind eye. Unfortunately for Degraves one of the officers was also a magistrate and so Degraves was immediately arrested for smuggling and taken to the New Bailey Gaol. It was only after the arrest that it was discovered that the goods had actually been stolen, so the charge was changed from smuggling to theft. Degraves claimed in his defence that he did not steal the goods, but that Parsons and others had swindled him and so he had merely tried to "… resolve the matter." However, Degraves' London clerk, Mr. Swan, testified in Court that he saw nothing in Bland's accounts that indicated a deliberate intention to swindle Degraves rather it was simply a series of compounded bookkeeping errors. Degraves was tried by a judge and jury, found guilty and sentenced to one year in prison, which he served in full. He was released in 1811 and less than a year later he received a full pardon. The reason for the pardon is not clear, but it was the first of a series of pleadings in which Degraves was able to mysteriously reverse or influence detrimental findings against him made by government officials. The fact that Degraves was involved in at least six court actions between 1805 and 1810 and spent a year in prison may account for the claims that he studied law. In truth he may have busied himself in such studies while in prison, rather than at the Inns of Court as he was later to claim. Whatever the case, he certainly found further use for legal studies through the remainder of his life for he was both a prolific litigant and a regular target for litigation. Degraves later stated in a letter to Governor Arthur, that, when he finally left England on the *Hope* in 1823, he was involved in numerous civil proceedings. These were under way in several courts around London and were at various stages of resolution upon which he expected to receive significant monies.

Over the next forty years of his life Degraves was to be imprisoned at least three more times and frequently became involved in both civil and criminal court cases.

Family Man
While Peter Degraves was attempting to grow a business empire in London and Manchester he was also establishing a family. Sometime around 1807, when as a bankrupt his goods and chattels were being sold off at the London Guild Hall to enable a dividend to be paid to his creditors, the 29 year old Peter Degraves married Sophia Macintosh, the 18 year old sister of Captain Hugh Macintosh his brother Henry's commanding officer in the Madras Native Infantry. Sophia was born in 1789,

Figure 6: Peter Degraves was imprisoned in Kings Bench, a London prison, which was very unlike how we would think of a prison today. Degraves' eldest son, Henry Degraves, who would later build Hobart's Theatre Royal, was conceived in Kings Bench Prison.

the daughter of an influential Inverness family.[43] It appears that her family moved from Scotland to England in the 1780s and settled in London where she and her brother Hugh were well educated in the Classics, reading both Latin and Greek. That her family allowed Sophia to be formally educated was relatively unusual for the early 19th Century.[44] Sophia's parents were undoubtedly well off as they were also able to afford the price of a cadetship for Hugh in the East India Company's army. Given Peter Degraves' propensity for concealing the truth it is unlikely that the 18 year old Sophia Macintosh or her parents knew he

---

[43] D. MacMillan *Scotland and Australia 1788 – 1850* (Oxford) 1967 p.85

[44] There is anecdotal evidence that while her husband was in prison in Hobart from 1826 to 1831 Sophia Degraves helped support her family by teaching from her home in Hobart.

was bankrupt at the time of their marriage. Sophia gave birth to the couple's first child, a girl also named Sophia, in July 1808; sadly she was either still born or died almost immediately after birth as she is listed as having been buried at Christchurch in Southwark on 9 July 1808.[45]

Peter and Sophia's next child, Louisa, was born in 1809. She was followed on the 29th April 1811 by their first son Henry. Both children were christened at the church of St George the Martyr in London, where Peter Degraves and his brother Henry had also been christened. Court documents surviving from his 1810 criminal trial indicate that, even after the failure of his business there, Degraves maintained a house in Manchester, but that his family home was in Cheapside in London. It is unlikely that these homes were owned by Degraves as he was still a bankrupt until at least July 1809, when dividends from the proceeds of the sale of his assets were being paid to his creditors. It is likely that his homes were owned by his Aunt or another family member, possibly even his wife; a common tactic employed by bankrupts in the 19th century and still in use today.

---

[45] Sophia ultimately had nine children; in 1816 she gave birth to another girl whom they also named Sophia.

Chapter Four: Highland Exile

Sometime during his year in prison Degraves was moved from the New Bailey Gaol in Manchester to London to be closer to his family, where he completed his sentence in King's Bench prison and was released at the end of 1811. Once released from jail he fled from London "Society" where, despite his eventual pardon, his ruined reputation would have made success in business almost impossible. Like his father before him, Degraves headed north to Scotland; though not to Edinburgh (where his half sister had been born).[46] Instead he headed for the Highlands where his wife's family had the necessary influence and connections that he would need to open doors for him. Degraves' first Scottish venture was on the Isle of Lewis in the Outer Hebrides, on the western frontiers of Scotland. Exactly why he chose the Outer Hebrides is not certain, though its distance from London would certainly have been a factor. It is also possible that Sophia's family had some connections or assets on Lewis which Degraves might have been able to utilise.

The Isle of Lewis is the main island of the Outer Hebrides off Scotland's west coast and is generally considered part of the Highlands. Originally Lewis was part of the domain of the Macleod clan, but was wrested from them in the late 16th century by the Mackenzies and by 1610 had become part of the Seaforth Estates, which were held by the chief of the Mackenzies, Lord Seaforth. On the Isle of Lewis Peter Degraves continued to chase his dream of making a great fortune, this time through a business scheme to cure large volumes of fish.[47]

---

[46] It is worth noting here that it is extremely likely that, by the beginning of the 19th century, Eliza Degravers had become closely acquainted with her father's other family as records from London's parish marriage registers show she and Malcolm Cowan were married at St Marylebone's church, only a few blocks from the Degraves' home in Red Lion Square, on 6 September 1807.

[47] A Fularton *The Topographical and Historical Gazetteer of Scotland.* Volume 1.

Whilst fish speculation in Scotland might seem a long jump from trading in French fabrics in London and Manchester, it contained the combination of wheeling and dealing and inventive engineering which seemed to have become part of Degraves' *modus operandi*. The fish-curing project also had another characteristic that suited Degraves, an obscure location that offered him the opportunity to make a fresh start and fast profits and where he could also either conceal or re-invent his past.

Around the time Degraves arrived on the Isle of Lewis (probably in 1813) fortunes had been made over the preceding decade selling cured meat and fish to the Army and Navy during Britain's extended war with Napoleon's forces. It is likely that Degraves saw there was a chance to use his technical genius (and whatever remaining capital he possessed) to make fast profits through industrialising the catching, curing and selling of large volumes of fish to the military. To this end Degraves hired a team of Dutch fishermen to man his boats and sent them to fish the seas around Lewis where prodigious quantities of fish could be caught quickly. It is not clear whether he built his own fish-curing factory or if he utilised an existing premises. Based on his track record and his later activities in Hobart, however, it was most likely that he built his own curing works by bringing in a local partner with either capital or property or both. It is also interesting that Degraves later claimed that at the time of the Battle of Waterloo he was working in the commissariat department in London, which, though extremely unlikely probably indicates that he had contacts in that department through whom he felt assured he would be able to guarantee the sale of his fish at a good price.

Although on paper the project appeared certain to succeed, Degraves' fishing enterprise was thwarted by a combination of bad timing, bad luck and his tendency to overreach himself. For just when his holding of stocks of cured fish was at its highest, the war with France ended and the price of all foodstuffs, particularly preserved meats such as salted beef and cured fish, plummeted by up to 90 percent. Degraves was thus left holding a vast stockpile of cured fish that was probably worth less than it had cost him to acquire.

After the collapse of his fishing venture Degraves either still owned or leased a coastal sailing vessel with which he was able to continue to trade in fish, whale oil and other goods. To make a profit he acquired marine produce from where ever he could around the Scottish coast then carried it by sea from the northern ends of the British Isles down to the busy markets in London. Thus in January 1819 he sailed from Stornaway, the main port on the Isle of Lewis, to London with a cargo that included a load of oil from 150 dolphins killed and distilled at Broad Bay on the Isle of Lewis. That he was forced to eke a living from such a humble trade did not dampen Degraves' ambitions for he had soon set his sights on other, grander, ventures.

Sometime before 1819 Degraves had decided that Stornaway, where he had originally set up his fish-curing enterprise, offered other opportunities that he might yet be able to exploit. He saw that the resources and the economy of Lewis were being poorly managed and, confident in his own genius, he was certain that he had the skills and vision to improve both through the use of his engineering and industrial skills whilst in the process making a handsome profit for himself. With these possibilities in mind he devised a fresh set of innovative projects that he succeeded in presenting to the new owners of the Isle of Lewis, Sir James Stewart-Mackenzie and his wife, Mary. James Alexander Stewart-Mackenzie was a well connected aristocrat, the son of Vice-Admiral Keith Stewart and the grandson of the 6th Earl of Galloway. However it was to Mrs Stewart Mackenzie, daughter and heir of the late Lord Seaforth, that the estate of the Isle of

Lewis belonged for Lord Seaforth had died leaving no surviving male heirs.[48]

The fate of the Seaforth Estate is part of Highland lore, which tells that in the early 17th century a curse was placed on the line of the chiefs of the Mackenzie clan by a Scottish seer named Kenneth Mackenzie.

Mackenzie, known as the Brahan Seer and often called the Scottish Nostradamous because of his ability to predict the future, his native Scottish Gaelic name was Coinneach Odhar, had been employed for some years by the then Lord Seaforth and his wife as their household prophet but when he gave a prophecy that greatly displeased Lady Seaforth (related to the fidelity of her husband who was, at the time, spending a few months in Paris) she had him executed on the charge of sorcery.

The mode of execution was by immersion in a barrel of boiling tar. The seer's last words were a curse that the last chief of the Mackenzie line would be deaf and dumb and would have four sons who predeceased him and that his estates would be brought to ruin. As the result of contracting scarlet fever in his youth the last Lord Seaforth, Francis Humberston Mackenzie, (who inherited the title after his elder brother was killed in a naval battle with the Marathas in India) was deaf and, for a period, dumb. He had four sons who all predeceased him, effectively ending the Seaforth/Mackenzie male line that had stretched back at least four hundred years.[49] After the death of Lord Seaforth in 1815, there being no male heirs, the title expired but the remains of the highly indebted estate passed to his recently widowed,

---

[48] In May 1817 Stewart married Lady Mary Hood, who was the widow of Admiral Sir Samuel Hood, and the eldest daughter of Francis Mackenzie – Lord Seaforth. Henceforth he took his wife's family name, thus becoming James Stewart-Mackenzie. Later in his varied career James Stewart-Mackenzie was appointed the Governor of Ceylon.

[49] P. Wilson 'Curse or Coincidence' *The North American Review* Vol. 230

eldest daughter, Lady Hood, formerly the wife of Admiral Hood. By the time that the estate reached Lady Hood she had re-married (1817) to James Stewart; however the Seaforth Estate (the Isle of Lewis in particular) had become a serious financial liability rather than the asset it should have been.

Figure 7: Mary Stewart-Mackenzie, widow of Admiral Hood, was a friend of Sophia Degraves (nee Macintosh). They were the same age and both from the small social circle of the Scottish Highland's upper classes.

The Isle of Lewis was a place where the relationship between landlord and tenant, as well as agricultural practices and culture, had been entrenched since ancient times. The predominant form of land use and occupation was the crofter system. Crofters paid an annual rent to the landlord for a set area of land, which was often shared with other crofter families who also shared the tasks of farming, gathering peat for fires or manning a small fishing boat. The rent was set arbitrarily by the landlord for his own benefit and was such that it enabled the crofter to sustain only the most basic of livelihoods.

The big problem for the Gallic speaking crofters of Lewis was that their children were reluctant to leave the island; and while the population grew the area of land shared amongst families did not. This shrinking of land-based resources was, to a degree, solved by exploiting the abundant resources of the sea. Initially this meant by fishing but by the late 18th century it also meant "kelping". By the beginning of the 19th century the population density on Lewis was about 40 persons per square mile (almost double that of the mainland), with the average family having to support itself on only an acre or two of land. This combination of overpopulation and overexploitation of the island's resources meant that more and more of those resources were used simply to maintain the growing population rather than generating cash flows into the economy.

Crofters lived in small, essentially self-sufficient, usually impoverished hamlets. The surrounding land was divided between families but "ownership" of each sub-division was generally rotated annually so that no crofter family exclusively owned land which was better or worse than any other member of the group. Agricultural practices were primitive, for example, wooden ploughs drawn by a team of four or five horses were still used in the mid 19th century. If agriculture was primitive in the Outer Hebrides so were the conditions in which the crofters lived. In the freezing, wet winters, they shared their dwellings ('black-houses') with their livestock. Constructed with a thick, low stone wall and a tall thatched roof, the black-houses were long and low and without windows or a chimney (smoke from the peat fires used for warmth and cooking seeped slowly out through the straw thatching of the roof). During the Napoleonic Wars, the Isle of Lewis had generated considerable income for Lord Seaforth's estate from sales of fish and kelp ash but the crofters saw little of this cash, forcing them to rely on agricultural and resource management practices that had not changed significantly in hundreds of years.

Kelp, which was washed up onto the shores of Lewis in huge quantities, had started to become an important source of income for Lord Seaforth from the mid-1780s. In the middle of the 18th century kelp ash, which was used in the rapidly growing industries of glass and soap manufacture, was fetching about £2 per ton. During the American Revolution it reached £10 per ton and peaked at £20 per ton in 1810. Lewis produced around 900 tons of kelp ash per anum for the Seaforth Estate so in 1810 kelp production alone would have been generating around £14,000 gross profit per annum for Lord Seaforth.

The kelp was gathered by crofters in the storm season when it was washed onto the beaches. On Lewis (as was the case in most of the islands and also the western Highland coastlines) the kelp was owned by the landlord, who paid the crofters at a set rate per ton for gathering the kelp. They then reduced the kelp to ash in crude ovens known as kelp kilns. The resulting product was sold by Seaforth around Britain, mostly to soap factories. As the price of kelp ash rose, the rate paid to the crofters remained the same, boosting profits to the point where they often exceeded the entire rental income of most Highland estates with west coast frontage. In the case of Lewis, it appears that the late Lord Seaforth had come to believe that the kelp income would never cease, for his needs became ever more extravagant, forcing him to borrow money against future income and mortgage his various holdings to fund his eccentric and excessive lifestyle. On his death in 1815 the Seaforth Estate was in a rare state of neglect and heavily in debt.

It was about this same time that Peter Degraves' fishing enterprise failed leaving the thrice failed entrepreneur to eke out a living by coastal trading. When, toward the end of the 19th century's second decade, Degraves saw the Seaforth estates pass to Lord Seaforth's daughter he also saw a chance for both profit and social advancement. It is likely that Degraves' wife, coming from a wealthy Highland family had the social connections that would have enable Degraves to have gained an introduction with the Stewart-Mackenzies. Once introduced Degraves set about trying to convince the new owner of Lewis, and her husband, that he could make the island a profitable part of their estates through a number of innovative development projects.

Degraves offered the new Laird and Lady a package of interesting, and genuinely advanced, ideas. These included building a factory which, he claimed, would be able to produce the industrial alkali, sodium carbonate, from salt rather than from kelp; constructing a reticulated town water supply for Stornaway; and making wholesale changes to the unhygienic black houses and inefficient farming practices of the Lewis Islanders. (Degraves' designed a more suitable and hygienic form of housing for both humans and livestock to eliminate the black houses as places for human residence, it was a valid plan that was ultimately not put into practice until the early 20th century.)

To Stewart Mackenzie Esquire 8th Jan 1819
Sir
I had occasion to pay another visit to Stornaway after I had the pleasure of seeing you there, and the weather being very fine and dry, and the inhabitants consequently much inconvenienced for want of water, I was consulted by several of them as to the best mode of furnishing a supply, and observing that most of the Wells occasionally become dry except for the Lodge Well, I thought that the best way would be to bring the water from Ault-na-Broag, down the hill close to the North side of the Plantation, and from thence in pipes under the Harbour opposite to Mr Angus Nicholson's house from whence pipes could be laid thro all the streets and by means of smaller pipes into every kitchen, which in the end is

much the cheapest way. But the first cost startled the people of Stornaway and they were in a state of uncertainty whether you had made any contract or not for laying on the water.

On the return of Mr McKinsie, your factor, they were informed that nothing as yet has been done on the business, I then made a survey of the Town and offered to lay down pipes according to my plan at my own expense upon certain conditions, the principle of which was that every Person should pay me 25 or 30 shillings per annum and when it was considered that a Public Tank (as before proposed) would be a mere gossiping rendezvous for servants who, in bad weather, would be subject to its inclemency as here to fore. Together with the same wear and tear of Buckets and that some of the inhabitants would have as great a distance to fetch it from the Tank as they now have to fetch it from the well. They came into my view of the thing and a meeting was held at the Mason's Lodge, where this subject was fully discussed and Captain McKinsie, Chairman of the Water Committee, has in consequence addressed a letter to you on the subject, which I should be happy to present in person if you are at no great distance and feel disposed to encourage my proposal, I shall be detained here for several days, my vessel having a cargo of Train Oil on board being part of the proceeds of 150 dolphins which were killed in Broad Bay in October while I was there; one of which I have preserved entire to present to the British Museum and in the event of you sanctioning my offer and being willing to grant me a perpetual lease of Ault-na-Broag, or such part of it as may be requisite for watering the Town of Stornaway, it will be advisable that I should see you personally before I go to London so that no delay may take place in preparing the necessary Legal arrangement.

Waiting your reply I have the Honour to be Most respectfully Yours

P. Degraves

Glasgow at Mr Alexander McNeil's   Wood Lane Broadmilan

From the various pieces of correspondence that have survived it seems that the new Mrs Stewart-Mackenzie and her husband initially entertained some interest in Degraves' plans and might have supported them had it not been that the estate was in such dire financial straits after the downturn in meat and fish prices and the continuing downward slide in the price of kelp ash. These factors, combined with the debts that the last Lord Seaforth had tied to the Estate on his death, severely reduced their available income and certainly curtailed investing in new schemes.

Interestingly it is likely that, had the Stewart-Mackenzies supported Degraves' scheme to establish a factory to convert salt to sodium carbonate, the fortunes of both may have been very different. For it is from Degraves' correspondence with James Stewart-Mackenzie that we have the first clear proof of Degraves' technical brilliance and his awareness of the latest scientific developments on the Continent. In a letter to Stewart-Mackenzie dated January 15th 1819 Degraves pointed out that the price of kelp ash was greatly over-inflated by the duty the British government placed on rock salt and would drop dramatically once that duty was removed. He went on to suggest that he could build a factory that could produce an industrial alkali from salt that was cheaper and at least three times more pure than the alkali made from kelp.

Degraves' prediction soon came true. Only four years later, after being progressively lowered, salt duties were dropped entirely and kelp prices tumbled to settle at around £3 per ton—approximately the cost of producing the kelp ash in the first place. Kelp prices never recovered from this level.[50]

As the steady income from kelp had been central to the fortunes of the Seaforth Estate for more than three decades, the decline in

---

[50] M Gray 'The Kelp Industry in the Highlands and Islands'

the price devastated the estate and by 1823 Stewart Mackenzie was forced to issue his own one pound notes as a means of remaining solvent. This dire strategy could well have been averted had he invested in the factory Degraves had suggested. By the mid-1820s those who had invested in similar ventures elsewhere in Britain were making huge profits supplying the rapidly expanding soap and glass industries.

Why Stewart-Mackenzie chose not to support Degraves' plan of bringing reticulated water to every house in Stornaway is not clear for Degraves indicated that he had the means to finance this venture himself, as he explained in the above letter. It was obvious that Degraves would quickly recoup his costs through the annual charge to each household of between 25 and 30 shillings per household. However as Degraves' plan involved laying a considerable amount of pipe from a lake in the hills above Stornaway as well as other major capital works, the combined cost would have been considerable so it must be assumed that Degraves had access to a substantial source of finance. In all likelihood this was probably, once more, his Aunt Deborah Decharme.

After at least one meeting and extensive correspondence with the Stewart-Mackenzies it must have become clear to Degraves that he would not receive the level of support that he needed to carry out his grand designs so he reverted to what appears to have been his 'Plan B'. This 'Plan B' involved moving himself and his rapidly growing family to somewhere even further from the scenes of his failures, somewhere there were opportunities for starting up another ambitious project; and far enough away from London for him to once more reinvent himself. Whilst the USA and Canada were amongst the options available to Degraves and other English emigrants it is clear that Degraves' investigations revealed to him that there was one place on Earth that was further away from Britain than any other place, but which still offered the benefits of British civilisation— Van

Diemen's Land. As the Australian colony with a climate most like England's, Van Diemen's Land had recently developed a reputation as a place where generous land grants and other incentives provided obvious opportunities for fast profits for an enterprising, smooth-talking, industrial entrepreneur like Degraves.

In the second decade of the 19th century, with the severe economic decline in the Scottish Highlands and the general trends to industrialisation across Britain, many British people, and particularly Scotsmen, were seeking to improve their fortunes in the Australian colonies and it is certain that Degraves would have heard numerous tales of the opportunities offered by this expanding new world—including those grants of vast tracts of land as well as access to free labour, in the form of convicts, and other benefits for men with capital and social connections. So it was to Van Diemen's Land that Degraves now planned to move himself and his family to make another fresh start and to have another attempt at making his fortune.

The only serious obstacle to this plan was the fact that Peter Degraves, rich in ideas, ambition and energy, was without capital or a means of transportation. However, never one to let an inconvenient truth block his plans, Degraves convinced his brother-in-law, Hugh Macintosh and his Aunt Deborah, to invest in the project. At Degraves suggestion Macintosh purchased the Bristol-built ship *Hope* from the Bristol-based shipping group Hooper & Co for the bargain price of £850. However bringing in his brother-in-law as a partner did not solve all of Degraves' problems for Macintosh was no fool and there is little doubt that he knew at least some of the history of Degraves' past, his failed projects and probably also knew that there were creditors again on Degraves' trail. For this reason Macintosh would not lend Degraves any cash and he also ensured that anything he purchased remained in his name. He also required that Degraves contribute equally, or close to equally, in terms of capital, either in cash or in kind. Degraves' lack of ready cash was exacerbated by the fact that creditors from his previous failed ventures still pursued him. In response to this new challenge the necessity to keep his plans of emigrating increased so Degraves embarked on a series of manoeuvres designed to obscure the nature of his activities and confuse the pursuing creditors. Part of these manoeuvres involved hiding any connection of his to the ownership of the *Hope* and the partnership planned for Van Diemen's Land.

Although existing histories claim that Degraves either fully owned or half owned the *Hope*, historic documents show conclusively that her only registered owner was Hugh Macintosh and that Macintosh was, and remained, her sole owner. [51] However it is a testament to the cleverness of Degraves' tactics they are still confusing historians in the 21st century, for most modern maritime histories indicate that the *Hope* was built in Venice, not Bristol, and was purchased from a London shipowner named Mr Duke, who was simply an associate of Degraves who he used as a front for his business transactions, if some such was needed.

The other issue which gives an insight into the ruthlessness of the relatively impoverished Degraves is how he raised the cash and acquired the milling machinery and other equipment he needed to take to Van Diemen's Land on board the *Hope* as part of his contribution to the Macintosh & Degraves partnership. (For Degraves put on board the *Hope* not only the materials and equipment to construct and operate a sawmill but also a complete steam engine.) This was a tangled affair, which will be dealt with in more detail in a following chapter, it is sufficient to say now that whilst ready cash was a serious problem for Degraves he did not let this become known and continued to live the life of an affluent gentleman. Using this

---

[51] Lloyds Shipping Registers: 1821 to 1827

ruse he was able to secure expensive machinery, tools and other equipment either on credit or by making a part payment on their delivery with the promise (which he had no intention of honouring) that the balance would be settled at some date in the near future.[52]

Whilst obtaining goods on credit helped him in some ways it did not solve all of Degraves' problems, there were some things that needed ready cash and ready cash was what he needed to achieve his goal of a new start in Hobart. Based on information revealed in letters from various of the *Hope*'s passengers in 1821, it is safe to say that Degraves would do whatever it took to get the money he needed to achieve his goals, even if it involved lying cheating and outright fraud; how he did this will also be discussed in a following chapter. Yet despite all Degraves' cunning manoeuvrings, creditors continued harassing him for payment of outstanding debts, right up to the moment that the *Hope* left England's shores in 1821, and would continue to do so for years to come, almost bringing about his total ruin, a ruin that would have been utterly final had it not been for the support of his wife and her brother Hugh Macintosh.

---

[52] Utas Archives M10/4/11

Section Two: Major Hugh Macintosh: the Honourable Mutineer

Chapter Five: The Company Cadet

When he died in Hobart, on Peter Degraves' birthday, at the end of 1834 Hugh Macintosh was the co-owner of the Cascades industrial complex which included saw mills, flour mills and a brewery; an enterprise he began with his brother-in-law, Peter Degraves, in 1824. Macintosh was also the sole registered owner of the *Hope* from 1821 to 1826. Without the monetary and moral support of Macintosh, neither the *Hope* nor Degraves would ever have made it to Hobart Town nor would the Cascades brewing empire ever have come into existence. Yet, despite the importance of Macintosh's contribution to the foundation of Cascades, little has been written about him. Even his obituary published in the *Hobart Courier* on 3rd of January 1835 was brief.

> Died at the Cascades on Wednesday 24th December 1834, Major Hugh Macintosh, formerly of H.E.I. Company's Service, and more latterly attached to the Persian Embassy, aged 58.

Yet despite the brevity of his obituary Macintosh actually led a life that was richer and more varied than that of his now renowned business partner, Peter Degraves.

Like Degraves, very little was known about Hugh Macintosh's early life other than that he was probably born in or near Inverness in late 1776. He certainly had one sibling, a sister named Sophia Macintosh who would later become Mrs Peter Degraves and it is likely that he had an older brother, although that is speculation, which will be discussed later. The seat of the Macintosh Clan lay in the lands around Inverness where Charles Macintosh owned agricultural property and his extended family had some significant influence, being engaged in a wide range of businesses. Australian historian David MacMillan states that Hugh Macintosh came from "an influential Inverness family" though he supplies no other information.[68]

It is known that the young Hugh Macintosh attended the exclusive Harrow School, a short distance north of London, from some time after 1780 through to 1790. In the late 18th century, and even today, Harrow and its traditional rival, Eaton, were considered to be the two most exclusive schools in England.

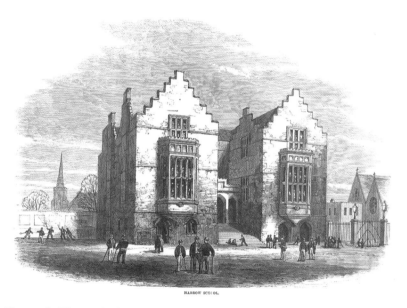

HARROW SCHOOL.

Figure 8: The exclusive Harrow School, where Hugh Macintosh formed a life long friendship with Henry Ellis, the illegitimate, but acknowledged, son of Lord Hobart, after whom Hobart Town was named.

At Harrow Hugh was given a classical education designed to prepare "young gentlemen" for the upper echelons of society.[69]

---

[68] David S MacMillan, *Scotland and Australia 1788-1850.* (Oxford) 1967
[69] C. Tyrerman *A History of Harrow School 1324-1991* (Oxford) 1990

During these years Macintosh became fluent in Latin and Greek, which, in his later life he taught to his sister Sophia's children in Hobart.[70] His talent with the Classical languages also appears to have given Macintosh a general love of learning languages which he used throughout his adult life, developing a reputation for fluency in a number of Asian languages, including Persian.[71] During his time at Harrow Macintosh made a number of lifelong friends, one of whom in particular, Henry Ellis, was to play a pivotal role in his future fortunes. Henry Ellis (later Sir Henry) was the acknowledged illegitimate son of the 4th Earl of Buckinghamshire, Lord Hobart, born in 1777 when the Earl was only seventeen, reputedly as the result of a youthful infatuation with a local village girl.[72] Whilst unable to inherit the title or fortunes of his father because of his birth outside of marriage, Henry Ellis grew up on his father's estates and rose to high levels in English society.[73] Blessed with great intelligence and, like his friend Macintosh, a gift for languages, Ellis led an extraordinarily interesting life which included two stints as British Ambassador to Persia as well as an appointment as Secretary to Britain's 1816 Embassy to China.

On the basis of Macintosh's attendance at Harrow it can be said that his immediate family were, if not members of the aristocracy, certainly wealthy and lived at a social level high enough to be able to send their son to such a prestigious school, for schools such as Harrow and Eaton did not accept just anybody as a student, one had to be socially connected. Macintosh's parents not only had to have the necessary high social standing needed to gain Hugh's entry to Harrow but also,

---

[70] E. Markham *Voyage to Van Dieman's Land* (London) 1834
[71] *Memorial of Hugh Macintosh to Lt. Governor Arthur* CSO1/281/6767
[72] W. Jones *Prosperity Robinson, the life of Viscount Goderich* (New York)
[73] W. Carpenter *Peerage for the People* (London) 1841

in 1790, to secure him the position of a cadet officer in the Honourable East India Company's Madras army.[74]

An appointment as an East India Company cadet required an interview with, and the direct patronage of, one of the Directors of the East India Company. As there were only 24 such directors, this not only required social connections but a substantial payment, which, for a military cadetship, was expected to be around £500. In the early 1790s these commissions were becoming very valuable because of the opportunities Company officers had for making considerable amounts of money on the side through various business deals, operating as agents or 'enforcers' for British business interests, and also through the collection of quasi legal taxes. These 'taxes' had been inherited by the H.E.I.C. officers when they took over the administration of many of towns and villages.

From around the middle of the 18th century the sons of genteel families who were intent on a military career had the choice of joining His Majesty's Army or the East India Company's army.[75] Their choice was often influenced by the financial status of the family for whilst being an officer in the Company's Army did not carry the social prestige or status of a similar rank in H.M. Army, the opportunities to amass significant wealth through "extracurricular" activities were considerable. This opportunity to make one's fortune as a Company army officer in India tended to attract a specific type of person sometimes

---

[74] Tyerman states that at the end of the 18th century Harrow was considered the second most popular and exclusive public school in Britain and as such was very selective about who was accepted as a student (Eton was the most exclusive).

[75] Through the period of Macintosh's life the terms Royal Army, King's Army or, more often, H.M. Army are used to distinguish between the Honourable East India Company's army and what would now be called the "regular" army. For consistency's sake I will use the term H.M. (His Majesty's) Army.

described as the "genteel poor" or "marginal middle class" who were often described with scorn by those of independent means. The Duke of York, in a letter to Indian Governor General, Lord Cornwallis, described the East India Company's officers thus:

> "The Officers are, in general, young men who have ruined themselves and are obliged to fly their Country, or very low people who are sent (to India) to make their fortunes, and who will therefore stick at nothing to gain money."

However such harsh criticism of the Company's officers was generally undeserved as they were, for the most part, well-educated young gentlemen whose only fault was that they either were not "first born sons" who could expect to inherit the family fortune or their families did not possess the vast fortunes of Britain's landed gentry and upper classes. In both these cases their families saw a cadetship in the East India Company as a sound investment in their son's and, often, their family's future. Indeed many Company officers rose to great wealth and respectability. The Duke of Wellington later wrote of them that:

> "… the desire to accumulate wealth and return to Europe is natural and praiseworthy in an officer of the local army in India."

And whilst the Duke of York and the officers of H.M. Army may have looked on the financial dealings of Company officers with disdain, it should be remembered that it was the expectation of profit that motivated all those involved with the East India Company's activities, particularly its shareholders, who more often than not were from the nobility or the upper classes and who sought a share in the great fortunes being made from the conquest of India. It is an interesting side note in this context that whilst 21 percent of officers in H.M. Army came from aristocratic families whereas in the East India Company's army this figure was only 4 percent.

Apart from these financial issues it is reasonable to say that the, often considerable, tensions generated between the officers of the Royal and Company armies were more a reflection of the different requirements imposed on them in the performance of their professional duties than any difference in the quality of the men themselves. And it can reasonably be said that it was the reliance on their wages and allowances that ultimately separated the Company's officers from the wealthy young gentlemen of independent means who became officers in H.M. Army. This dependence on wages and allowances by the Company's officers was a factor that was to profoundly shape Hugh Macintosh's life.

Another fundamental difference between the two British armies occupying India was that in His Majesty's Army young officers could progress upward through the ranks on the basis of whether or not they or their parents could afford to purchase a promotion when one became available, whereas in the Company's army one had to rely on connections, merit and the death or promotion of a superior officer. This meant that the incompetent son of a wealthy aristocrat could, at a young age, rapidly gain a high rank in His Majesty's Army whereas in the Company's army a highly qualified and competent officer could languish in a low rank for many years waiting for someone to die before he received a deserved promotion.

Another feature of officers in the H.M. Army was that it was often the case that the wages they received were largely irrelevant when compared to the family monies and allowances to which they had access. This financial independence allowed His Majesty's officers to focus their attentions on abstract martial ideals such as honour, courage and attaining prestige amongst their peers, rather than being constantly on the lookout for monetary advantage or developing local relationships with India traders, which in turn meant that the officers in the Company's army tended to have much closer personal connections with the local Indian population. It therefore followed that while Company officers also professed to hold to the same martial ideals as their Royal Army counterparts, they often found that their actions and energies came to be focused on more pragmatic issues, such as acquiring their fortunes and ensuring their entitlements, in a way which might potentially compromise their martial ideals; in fact, most of the problems that the Company had with its army revolved around exactly these issues.

When Hugh Macintosh joined the Honourable East India Company's Army as a cadet officer in 1790, aged 14, it was at a time when the Company's relationship with its Indian army was going through a process of significant change that would ultimately result in the Company wielding a more professional and powerful force, with which it would subjugate the Indian sub-continent. Part of this process was the decision to improve the training of its officers. This formal training program eventually resulted in the establishment of a dedicated cadet academy in England in the early 19th century; however as this occurred after Macintosh's time the young Macintosh completed his cadetship at the military academy at Deptford where both Company and H.M. Army cadet officers were trained to meet the increasing demand for European officers in India.

To better understand the reason for the East India Company's evolving military policies, policies that were to have an important effect on the course of Hugh Macintosh's life, it is worth having a short look at how the Company's army developed. For the first part of the 18th century the East India Company's army was relatively small and was manned predominantly by British and European troops, primarily engaged in protecting the Company's interests and assets in India. There was little interest in using the local population in a military capacity as the British considered Indian soldiers to be inferior to their own, a position supported by the numerous easy victories European troops had over Indian forces. However, in 1756 Robert Clive convincingly demonstrated the value of a well-trained native army when, with just 800 troops (300 Europeans and 500 native troops, known as sepoys), he seized the fortified city of Arcot and then defended it against a combined enemy force of over 10,000 French and Indian troops. As Clive's influence in India grew his recommendations and examples were followed so that in the years following the battle at Arcot the Company embarked on an extensive program of training native soldiers for service in what became known as the Native Infantry. The native Infantry became a deadly force and, although the sepoys were generally considered to be superior soldiers to those of European origin because of their familiarity with the climate and living conditions, they were paid much less than Europeans and always kept under the command of European officers. Getting more for less was a situation that suited the East India Company very well.

When Macintosh took up his cadetship the East India Company's Indian army was essentially two armies within one. There were regiments made up mostly of British- born soldiers, referred to as the European army, and there were regiments made up of native Indians, known as the Native Infantry. As well as getting significantly less pay than their European counterparts, within the Native Infantry there was no opportunity for Indians, regardless of their abilities, to rise above the level of sergeant, whilst in the European army talented individuals could rise up through the ranks to the highest positions. [76] This essentially racist Company policy also excluded from the possibility of attaining officer rank all persons of mixed race (Anglo-Indian parentage) regardless of

---

[76] D. Peers 'Between Mars and Mammon: the east India Company and Efforts to Reform Its Army' *The Historical Journal* Vol. 33 No. 2, 1990.

the social or military status of the parents.[77] For example Peter Degraves' brother Henry married an Indian woman so, even though Degraves was a Lieutenant-Major and a 'gentleman', any son from the union could never have aspired to be an officer in the Indian Army.

The European regiments had been originally intended to ensure that there was a loyal British core to the Company's military presence in India, while the European soldiers were expected to set an example of "Britishness" for the native forces. However as the 18th century progressed it became increasingly difficult for the Company to attract suitable British men as troops for its Indian Army. As the British portion of their forces decreased the Company's directors, as well as its officers in India, became extremely concerned about the numerical imbalance and, over the years, attempted a series of strategies to reverse the chronic shortage of European personnel.

This recruiting problem was primarily due to the series of wars in which Britain was involved during the latter portion of the 18th Century, most notably the Seven Year War and the American Revolution. Because H.M. Army was pressed for troops during this extended period of war, the East India Company was seen by it as a competitor and the government legislated in favour of His Majesty's Army. Amongst other things this resulted in the East India Company being prohibited from recruiting new troops "by the beat of the drum". Recruiting "by the beat of the drum" refers to the practice of sending out a Captain and/or a sergeant with the regiment's colours as well as pipers and drummers, all resplendently done up in dress uniform, to visit country towns and villages. Once a crowd had been gathered by the pipes and drums, the captain or sergeant would address the crowd with glowing descriptions of the benefits of

---

[77] M Fisher 'Excluding and Including Natives of India: early 19th Century Race Relations in Britain.' *Comparative Studies of South Asia, Africa*

Army life. As well as a regular salary, excitement and glory potential recruits were offered a monetary bounty "the King's shilling" when they signed up.

As their army became increasingly short of British soldiers, and with no other obvious options, the Company directors decided to resort to the practice of "crimping". The practice of crimping involved a professional crimper who was paid a bounty for each man delivered to the Company's premises by whatever means. Crimping resulted in a range of abuses from gross misrepresentation of the pay and conditions in the Company's army to outright kidnapping, whilst the "per head" bounty led to the crimps being completely indiscriminate in whom they "enlisted". The easiest pickings were the "riff raff" of London's back streets and even prisoners in jail for minor offences. For example, by paying a fine or a bribe that was less than the bounty a crimper could acquire a number of prisoners jailed for minor offences and transfer them directly to the Company's holding yards.

In 1787 India's Governor General Lord Cornwallis expressed his low opinion of the European troops arriving at the Indian garrisons in a letter to the Duke of York. As he put it "…the contemptible trash of which the Company's European force is composed makes me shudder."

Once the crimps had got their men they were placed in Company lock-ups near the docks where they were held until their ship was ready to sail.[78] Yet even when the Company had acquired a sufficient number of British troops to send on to India, that manpower was further reduced by the terrible conditions encountered on the long passage, often lasting six months. Deaths and extreme illness due to scurvy and other shipboard

---

[78] A. Gilbert 'Recruitment and Reform in the East India Company Army 1760-1800' *Journal of British Studies* Vol. 15 No.1 1975 pp.91-95

maladies were such that even those that survived the voyage were often incapable of taking up their duties as soldiers.

By the mid 1780s growing public opposition to the East India Company's recruitment methods, and the realisation by its directors that their recruitment practices were ultimately deterring suitable men from considering a serious career in the Indian Army, encouraged a process of reform. A series of changes were made between 1786 and 1796, which included the requirement by the Company that the British government change legislation to allow the Company to gather recruits "by the beat of the drum". This eliminated the need for crimpers and increased both the number and quality of recruits. Another change was to increase the numbers of Native Infantry, which in turn required a larger body of professionally trained British officers to ensure that the native regiments were "properly" commanded. This also combined with a general trend for increasingly intensive cadet training programs in most of Europe's armies as armies became more industrialised. It was into this system of professional officer training that Hugh Macintosh entered at Deptford. (Previous to this period cadet officer training had involved an informal type of apprenticeship between young men and existing officers where it was assumed that by simply drawing officers from the ranks of "gentlemen's sons" that their social rank and "breeding" would naturally and automatically give them the necessary qualities required in an officer.)

Macintosh completed his cadetship, which also included lessons in the Persian and Hindu languages, in August 1791 and was promoted to the junior rank of second lieutenant. He had just turned sixteen when he sailed on a Company ship to Madras, where Lord Hobart, the father of his school friend Henry Ellis, was soon to take up the governorship.[79]

---

[79] Lord Hobart was Governor of Madras from 1794 to 1798.

Leaving England, the young Macintosh would have stood on the deck of the one of the Company's huge East Indiaman, massive ships designed to carry both passengers and goods, generally measuring between 1100 and 1400 tons, more than four times the size of Cook's ship *Endeavour*. So valuable were the East Indiamen, laden with spices, silks and other goods from the East, that they were often painted to resemble warships with additional gunports painted onto their hull so an attacker could not be sure if gunports were real or not. Subterfuge aside they also carried sizeable armaments.

Figure 9: A typical ship of the East India Company upon which Hugh Macintosh spent more than five months sailing from England to Madras

Even though Company officers travelled in comfortable conditions on an East Indiaman the young Macintosh would have watched England's shores fading in the distance whilst wrestling with his feelings as he contemplated his farewell to his parents and his little sister Sophia (who would have been less than five years old). He knew that if he ever saw any of them again it would not be for at least a decade, which was the minimum period of service before an officer was granted leave. He would also have known that there was a reasonable chance he would be dead before that time was up or that, if he did eventually return to Britain, it might be as an invalid, disabled by injury or disease. Approximately ten percent of the Company's European troops died every year, though the main cause of death amongst the soldiery was not war wounds, but venereal diseases. Struggling with homesickness young Macintosh would also have had to deal with the "...horrors of seasickness" which, as another young cadet wrote, "... is of itself enough to make a man wish he were at the bottom of the deep sea."

But these were all issues that every man, woman or child, officer, soldier or convict leaving Britain for any distant land would have had to endure. However, unlike the soldiery, as an officer and the son of a gentleman aboard an East Indiaman the young Hugh Macintosh would have travelled in relative comfort with his own cabin (or perhaps he may have shared a cabin with another cadet) and dined at the Captain's table with reasonable regularity. As the voyage from England to Madras took between five and six months, Macintosh would have formed his first batch of new relationships aboard the ship. Captain Charles Blakiston, who made the same journey a decade after Macintosh, also as a Company cadet, described the mixture of persons that a young officer might expect to find for company aboard an East Indiaman:

> The generality of our society on board was respectable, and some of its members were men of great education and talent. Excepting that there was no lady in the party it was composed of the usual materials found around the cuddy-table of an East Indiaman…

These "materials" included a judge, several high ranking officers, junior officers and a number of civilian Company employees, some travelling to India for the first time and some returning to India after taking a year or two's furlough in Britain. With such a varied company Macintosh would have spent his days playing cards, walking the decks while discussing various topics with his peers and seniors, playing pranks or simply reading. It would be certain that the "old hands" aboard would have given a large amount of attention to preparing the young men for the realities of life in India.[80]

---

[80] C. Blakiston *Twelve Years' Military Adventure* (London) 1829 pp. 19-23

Figure 10: Fort Saint George, where Hugh Macintosh was stationed on arrival, was the centre of British power in Madras and Southern India.

Chapter Six: Madras and Mysore

After more than five months at sea, sighting Madras and the palm-studded coastline of south east India must have been a powerful experience for all on board, particularly those who, like Macintosh, had never previously left British shores. Once on shore Macintosh was expected to find his own way through Madras to Fort St George, the headquarters of the East India Company's army in Madras. Most likely he would first have, like Blakiston, taken a room in a hotel in town for a night or two to refresh himself and regain his "land legs" before walking to the gates of the fort and then through and over a "… succession of outworks and drawbridges and a number of angular walls and deep moats" before eventually reaching the officer to whom he had to present his credentials. No doubt Macintosh would have been struck, like Blakiston, by the observation that, despite the searing tropical heat, the soldiers and officers he met were all in full uniform with their coats buttoned up to their chins.[81] Once the necessary paperwork had been completed Macintosh was assigned to the Cadet Company where he spent several months with the other newly arrived cadets learning what was expected of a young officer of the Madras Native Infantry. Eventually the time came when he was assigned to his own regiment to begin his duties as a junior officer in the Company's Madras Army's. Macintosh was placed in the 1st Battalion of the 8th Regiment of the Native Infantry and would stay with, and soon command, that battalion for his entire time in India, almost 20 years.

Figure 11: A young officer of the East India Company's Madras Army

[81] C. Blakiston *Twelve Years' Military Adventure* (London) 1829

Behind the city of Madras, to the west, lay the extensive Hindu kingdom of Mysore. Until 1792, the year of Macintosh's arrival, this kingdom had stretched across most of the southern end of India from just outside of Madras on the east coast all the way over to the west coast. Mysore was ruled by a man named Tipu Sultan; most people would have considered Tipu Sultan a despot however, in the context of his time he was simply an extremely powerful and ambitious ruler.

Whilst ostensibly a Hindu kingdom, Mysore had been controlled since the 1760s by Muslim rulers who had usurped the authority of Mysore's Raja, who was, however, retained as a figurehead of the government. This overthrow was initially carried out by Tipu Sultan's father, Hyder Ali, who, though illiterate, was a highly intelligent and skilled political and military tactician. Although Hyder Ali was the son of a general in the service of the Raja of Mysore he worked his way up through the ranks of Mysore's army to become the Raja's Prime Minister. Not long after becoming Prime Minister Hyder Ali staged a coupe, deposed the Raja and seized complete power over Mysore in 1763, after which he devoted most of his time and energy using his army to expand the size of his newly acquired realm. He rapidly and ruthlessly expanded westward to conquer the small kingdoms and communities of India's south west coast after which he shifted his attentions to the east where he clashed with British interests as he moved closer to Madras. The East India Company was well aware that Hyder Ali both recognised the threat of British intrusion into Mysore and resented the increasing influence of the British in India generally. They also knew that he had vowed to drive them from the sub-continent. To facilitate this ambition Hyder Ali had formed an alliance with Britain's traditional enemies, the French. Over the following decades a series of fierce engagements were fought between Hyder Ali and the British (or their Indian allies) with significant victories and defeats for both sides. This almost constant warfare resulted in enormous losses in terms of money and personnel for the East India Company.

An insight into the nature of the war between Hyder Ali and the British and also an insight into the life led by Hugh Macintosh during this per... ...going warfare can be given by including the story of another young Scottish officer who arrived in Madras almost ten years before Macintosh, Captain David Baird, who, like Macintosh was a Highlander.

Immediately on his arrival in Madras, Captain Baird was attached to the force, commanded by Sir Hector Munro, which was sent to assist a detachment the Company's army being threatened by Hyder Ali's forces.

Figure 12: This portrait of Hyder Ali, circa 1760's, drawn by a French artist, not long after Hyder Ali seized control of Mysore's throne.

Baird's company was sent forward to join another detachment under the command of Colonel Baillie but they were intercepted and surrounded by the combined forces of Hyder Ali and his son Tipu. The British immediately came under a destructive bombardment from Hyder's cannon and rockets. The survivors of the artillery fire were then attacked by Tipu's cavalry of horses and elephants as well as the infantry of Hyder Ali, who kept up an incessant fire of musketry. The British force was now decimated and Colonel Baillie, seeing further resistance was hopeless, tied his white handkerchief on his sword as a flag of truce, and ordered Baird (second in command) to cease firing. The truce was apparently granted, but as soon as the British had laid down their arms, Tipu's cavalry, himself at their head, rushed upon them, cutting down every man within their reach. Baird, whose company was literally cut to pieces by this attack received two sabre wounds to the head, a bullet in his thigh, and a pike-wound in his arm and fell senseless to the ground amongst the dead and dying. The enemy moved through the wounded killing any who remained alive, removing heads for trophies as they went. Fortunately night fell before they reached Baird so that he and a few others were able to crawl from the slaughter under the cover of darkness.

Wounded and exhausted Baird and four other officers with him were eventually captured by the French and handed over to Hyder Ali who decided to keep them as hostages and so imprisoned them in the dungeons deep in the stone bowels of Seringapatam. The still wounded Baird was shackled to the dungeon's walls in iron fetters weighing more than 5 kilos, with his maggot infested wounds adding to the horror of his confinement.

Early in the period of Baird's imprisonment, in December 1782, Hyder Ali died of cancer during a Monsoon induced interlude in his war against the British near Madras. Hyder Ali's death brought no relief to Baird or the East India Company as Hyder was immediately succeeded by his son, Tipu, who took the title of Sultan of Mysore. Tipu ensured that Baird remained chained in his dungeons for four years and Baird was only eventually released as part of a treaty that brought a temporary peace between Tipu and the British.

Figure 13: Captain Baird after his release from four years in Tipu Sultan's dungeons in the fortress, Seringapatam. Baird would later ask to lead the British forces' charge into the breach in Seringapatam's walls.

In contrast to his father, Tipu Sultan was extremely well educated but although a forward and innovative thinker he was not as skilled in the arts of war or diplomacy and suffered greatly from over confidence. Because Tipu tended to be erratic and because there have been recent attempts to "redeem" or to " re-assess" him as a freedom fighter against British

Imperialism, descriptions of Tipu's character are often contradictory. He was given the honorific of "The Tiger of Mysore" and, like his father, is generally acknowledged to have been a fierce and fearless warrior. There were two other things that Tipu held in common with Hyder Ali. One was his absolute power as the ruler of Mysore and the other was his hatred of the British. One of his favourite possessions was a life sized mechanised tiger crouched atop a prostrate British soldier given to him by the French. The clockwork tiger continually acted out the killing of the soldier. Tipu also kept real tigers in his palace at Seringapatam to which he was not averse to feeding with his enemies.

Tipu Sultan continued to ruthlessly prosecute hostilities against British interests and allies around the borders of his kingdom over the next ten years until the British, under Governor General Lord Cornwallis, decided to launch a full scale attack to finally remove this obstacle to British expansion in India. Cornwallis initially moved toward Tipu with a force of around 20,000 men from both His Majesty's army and the Company's army; to this force, as it progressed across Mysore, was added a horde of cavalry from various Indian allies and further troops from the kingdom of Hyderabad as well as another British 6,000 soldiers from the Malabar Coast.

This huge force reached the city of Seringapatam in February 1792 where Cornwallis found a heavily fortified city that occupied an island in the Kaveri River. The city proper occupied the centre of the island around and upon which Tipu had arrayed an army of at least forty thousand men.

After some heavy fighting Tipu was eventually defeated in the first ever siege of his capital; these events took place at about the same time as the young Hugh Macintosh arrived in Madras to take up his post as a junior officer in the Native Infantry so that his first experience of India was filled with the news of the

British victory as well as tales of glory and riches won in the battle.

Figure 14 A young Tipu Sultan, painted about the time he assumed the rule of Mysore after the death of his father Hyder Ali

Whilst the period after Macintosh's arrival in Madras is most notable because it saw the apparent end of the threat from Tipu Sultan it also saw the beginning of the end of another set of problems that had plagued the Company's operations in Madras. During the last quarter of the 18th century systemic corruption had combined with the constant threat of war to almost cripple the Company's Madras business and reduce its revenue flows to almost zero. The fact that the Company's highest ranking civilian and military officers were more intent on enriching themselves than serving their employer appropriately, severely limited the Company's military and commercial capacity. The situation in Madras had begun to improve after the arrival of Lord Cornwallis in 1786 and his subsequent defeat of Tipu Sultan. The terms demanded by Cornwallis for Tipu Sultan's surrender required Tipu to give over to the Honourable East India Company half of his kingdom plus three million pounds sterling in gold and silver coin (about $5 billion in today's money). These terms and the effective intervention of Cornwallis in Madras affairs so altered the Company's position there that the period immediately after the initial defeat of Tipu Sultan is generally considered to have been of pivotal importance to Britain's eventual supremacy in India. Suddenly the East India Company had gone from controlling a medium-sized, poorly administered city in the South of India to possessing half of Mysore—a kingdom about the same size as England with relatively sized revenue streams. The administration and garrisoning of such a vast territorial asset required a considerable injection of manpower. As a result, as well as military duties, many additional administrative tasks also fell to the Company's army officers. It was a good time to be an officer in the Company's army; fortunes could be, and were, made.

Meanwhile, across the whole of the Indian sub-continent, the ingress of various European powers into Indian society had resulted in the destabilisation of the traditional Indian territorial boundaries and the associated hierarchies. As well as the British, the Dutch, French, Portuguese and Danes were all represented in various port cities around the Indian coastline, all seeking to grab a share of the wealth of India by any means possible. It was, however, the East India Company's interventionist policies in Indian political life that had the most profound effect. These policies were designed to "divide and conquer" by exaggerating and exploiting the developing social instability and traditional rivalries. This approach was successful to the point where many of the Indian rulers were either toppled directly by the Company militarily or were conquered indirectly through the supply of military support to a rival. The victorious rival was then required to grant the Company favourable trading terms or other rights when he gained power. Such support, and the continuing military presence that went with it, was called a "subsidiary", and it always involved the Company 'insisting' that its new ally accept the ongoing protection of the Company's army, which was then garrisoned at strategic places within the new ally's territory. This was actually a sophisticated type of protection racket which effectively created either vassal or tributary states. The Company's allies, whilst nominally acknowledged as the rulers of their domains, were forced to pay for the Company's military protection through the impost of a significant annual fee which was intended to both cover the Company's military expenses and to make it a profit. Thus, after the death of Tipu Sultan the East India Company installed one of the sons of the rightful Raja of Mysore as ruler. The Raja was then required to pay the Company £280,000 annually for the ongoing "protection" of the Company's army. The additional gain from this policy was that the Company's troops were always garrisoned at the best fortified locations from which, should the necessity arise, it could enforce any disputes with, or breaches of contract by, its allies. Once again the Company expected the officers of its army to carry out these combined military and administrative duties, which provided the officers with further opportunities for pecuniary gain through claims for allowances and various unofficial "taxes" on the local population.

Because the demands upon the Company's Madras army expanded after the first defeat of Tipu Sultan the H.E.I.C. had to significantly increase the troop numbers of both its European and Native armies. However, as the numbers of recruits that could be brought from Britain was relatively limited, and their death rate, once in India, was high, the Company Directors decided to build up their Native Infantry. Native troops offered the Company a double advantage, as wages (generally as much as one tenth of the rate paid to European soldiers) and other expenses were lower while the number of potential recruits was much greater. It only required that there be sufficient recruiting and training of British-born officers to command the expanding Native Infantries. Through the early 1790s, when Hugh Macintosh arrived in India, this shortage of European troops meant that of a combined force of over 70,000 soldiers in the Company's India army only about 6,000 were Europeans.

When the Native Infantry was originally established each regiment was overseen by only three European officers: a commandant, who was usually a captain, and two subalterns, usually lieutenants. Beneath the European officers there was also a European sergeant. Generally the highest rank a sepoy could have aspired to during the period of Clive's Native Infantry was that of corporal. However, the structure of the Native Infantry was reorganised with the reforms of 1786 and 1796 which made it possible for Sepoys to rise to the rank of sergeant. The same reforms also saw the Native Infantry divided into regimental structures more in line with those of the H.M. Army, with each regiment consisting of two battalions and the number of officers overseeing the troops of each regiment being brought up to around the same ratio as in the regulars. This meant that each native regiment was usually commanded by a Colonel with the battalions of five hundred sepoys under the control of a captain, a major or a lieutenant colonel, with two or more junior British officers beneath them. [82] This was the structure of the Madras army when the young Hugh Macintosh arrived.

After completing his time in the Cadet Company, Macintosh was posted into the 1st Battalion of the 8th Regiment of the Madras Native Infantry as the battalion's most junior European officer; and even as a 16-year-old he still had complete authority over the most senior native soldier in the battalion of about 500 men of various levels of training and rank. The combination of the expansion of the Company's territories and the numerous minor conflicts that were occurring at this time offered opportunities for rapid promotion so that in February 1794, aged just 18, Macintosh, who must have demonstrated a high degree of competence in his job, was promoted to a full Lieutenant. However it was not until the beginning of 1799 and the advent of the final, decisive battle between British forces and Tipu Sultan, at Seringapatam, that we gain a clear view of the character of Hugh Macintosh and the experiences that were to shape him into the man he would become.

---

[82] A. Cardew *The White Mutiny* (Bombay) 1929 p.14

Figure 15: Although only 16 years old Lt. Macintosh was ranked above any Sepoy in his battalion, regardless of age or experience. Over the next 20 years Macintosh would gain the respect and loyalty of his troops as he risked his own life and, ultimately his career, leading them into battle.

Chapter Seven: The Siege of Seringapatam and the Marathas Wars.

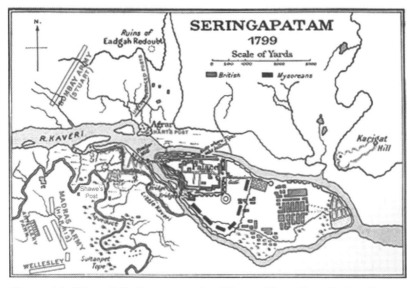

Figure 16: Map of Seringapatam by fellow officer Captain Blakistone. Macintosh was stationed at Shawe's Post, shown above, and led his troops through the trenches (red zig zag) from Shawe's Post to the river.

Following his defeat by Cornwallis in 1792 and no longer able to prosecute his habitual battles with his neighbours, Tipu Sultan reverted to spending most of his time in, or around, his capital city, Seringapatam, hunting and scheming; scheming the defeat of the hated British.

Built on a rugged granite island in the middle of the Kaveri River Seringapatam was an ideal fortress city with high stone walls surrounded by water. After his 1792 defeat, as well as rebuilding and strengthening the city's massive walls Tipu dug deep, wide trenches into the granite bedrock behind the walls. He also began a discreet but relentless program of acquiring a mass of weaponry for his final battle with the British. With the help of his French allies Tipu purchased firearms and cannon from Europe as well as making his own cannon and muskets in local foundries. Interestingly, he also created a huge arsenal of military rockets and trained troops of "rocketeers" to fire them at enemy targets, usually cavalry. [83] To train his troops Tipu employed approximately 400 French soldiers who were under the command of Colonel Louis Chappuis, who was also one of Tipu's chief military advisors.

Figure 17: Tipu Sultan at the time of the Siege. Tipu fought bravely in the front line and died with his sword in his hand, fighting as he fell.

Events turned further to Tipu's favour when, in 1795, his enemy Lord Cornwallis was replaced as Governor General by a long-serving Company bureaucrat, Sir John Shore, who, though a competent administrator, lacked the military and diplomatic

---

[83] L. Bowering *Haidar Ali and Tipu Sultan* (London)1893

experience of his predecessor.[84] During Shore's term of office (1795-98), Tipu continued his preparations for war against the British unhindered. He also sent emissaries to Persia, Afghanistan, Turkey and other Islamic nations in an attempt to enlist their support in his plans of jihad against the hated British.

In 1798 Shore was replaced by the aristocrat Lord Richard Wellesley (Lord Mornington), supported by his two brothers, Henry and Arthur (Arthur Wellesley became Tipu's, then Napoleon's, nemesis, the Duke of Wellington). When Lord Mornington spies made him aware of Tipu's plans to break the 1792 treaty Mornington sent letters by his personal emissary to the Sultan's court seeking clarification of the 'rumours' and a confirmation of their treaty. On realising that Mornington knew what he was planning Tipu overestimated the strength of his position and treated Mornington's emissary with a disdain calculated to insult both the emissary and Lord Mornington and to bring on the confrontation with the British that he had long desired. Unfortunately for Tipu Sultan Mornington, as he received more and more intelligence of Tipu's activities, obliged by deciding to settle the matter immediately, by military means.

Lord Mornington gathered a massive offensive force, which he described as "… the finest army that ever took the field in India". His plan called for joining the East India Company and Royal armies in the East, stationed in Bengal and Madras, with His Majesty's Army forces stationed in Bombay in the North West. The combined force of around 37,000 fighting men (of which about 30,000 would be supplied by the East India Company) was to meet outside the walls of Seringapatam in the Spring of 1799. Spring was chosen because it offered a climatic window where temperatures were not oppressive and was prior to the commencement of the monsoons when rainfall would make the

---

[84] E. Thompson & G. Garratt *Rise and Fullfillment of British Rule in India*

movement of a large army across India's landscape almost impossible.

It was as part of this force that Lieutenant Macintosh and his battalion left Madras to join in the battle that would establish the East India Company as the "power paramount" in India. As Macintosh marched his battalion toward Seringapatam from the east, another man who would also later play an important part in Australian history, Major Lachlan Macquarie, marched toward the same destination from the west. A future Governor of New South Wales, Macquarie was part of the His Majesty's Bombay Army and a member of the combined armies' commander General Harris's staff. Several accounts of the Siege of Seringapatam, particularly one by Major Alexander Beatson, provide enough information to follow Macintosh's progress through this historic battle.[85] However, unfortunately, as all the accounts were written by officers of the Royal Army the accounts are highly Anglo-centric and generally tend to ignore the contribution of Company's Native Infantry and its officers even though the Company's forces were in the front of, and active in, all the battles of Seringapatam.

Hugh Macintosh reached Seringapatam on the 4th April 1799 and settled his battalion, part of the 5th Brigade under Colonel Roberts, into the base camp that the forward party had established about three kilometres from the city, just beyond effective range of the many cannon Tipu had mounted on Seringapatam's towering granite walls. While the camp was being organised General Harris ordered the surrounding countryside be made secure. As part of these orders another man who was to build his military reputation on the battlefields of India, Colonel Arthur Wellesley, was given command of a column that included His Majesty's 12th regiment, under the command of Colonel Shawe, and two battalions of Sepoys—

---

[85] Macquarie's journal is available on-line from the Mitchell Library

Macintosh's 1st battalion and another from the 3rd Regiment of Native Infantry. This company was ordered to make a night time attack to clear an area about half way between the British camp and the city, where enemy forces were ensconced amongst several ruined villages, rocky hill tops and irrigation ditches dug in the stony ground and from where they were able to fire rockets and musket balls into the British camp.

Under cover of darkness Macintosh's battalion made their way up the hillside but were seen and attacked by enemy forces hiding in one of the ruined villages. After a short, fierce battle Macintosh's men secured the ruins only to be pinned down by enemy musket and rocket fire from the main irrigation channel, about 40 metres above the village, where the enemy forces had been reinforced.

Meanwhile Colonel Wellesley (later the Duke of Wellington), seeing Macintosh's men were trapped, brought his force up on the flank of the channel to create a diversion. Seeing the enemy distracted by the flank attack Colonel Shawe led Macintosh and his men out of the ruins in a bayonet charge at the irrigation channel. The combination of flank and direct attack routed the enemy forces from this area but in the mêlée Wellesley and his men became lost in the dark and accidently moved deeper into enemy territory where they were ambushed by a strong force of Tipu's retreating soldiers. In the almost total darkness it was difficult to tell friend from foe and many of Wellesley's men were shot or captured. Wellesley himself was wounded in the knee by a musket ball and would have been captured if not for the intervention of Macintosh and his battalion, who hearing the sounds of battle rushed to his aid and saved the future hero of the Napoleonic Wars from death, or worse.

Although the capture of this strip of territory had almost ended in disaster for Wellesley it did ensure a special place in the future Duke's heart for the East India Company's native infantry and in particular for Macintosh's 1st Battalion which was thereafter known as "Wellesley's Battalion". A further result of Wellesley's rescue was that Macintosh and his 1st Battalion accompanied Wellesley (who was rapidly promoted to General) on all his major campaigns in India.[86] However the capture of the high ground above the camp was clearly Colonel Shawe's victory and the hill became known as Shawe's Post, which created a secure front line from where the British Army could build its cannon batteries and trenches. Shawe's Post was permanently manned by H.M. 12th Regiment and Macintosh's battalion of Native Infantry.[87]

An artillery battery for two 12 pound cannon was built on the hill at Shawe's Post and was guarded, in rotation, by the troops who had captured it, meaning Macintosh would have periodically been in command of this post. Tipu's forces launched regular attacks on Shawe's Post, which caused considerable casualties for both sides, although none of Tipu's attacks were effective in delaying the British. On 22nd April Macintosh led his battalion forward again to take control of a deep ravine about 600 metres closer to the walls of Seringapatam, within easy range of Tipu's cannon, where another battery for two 12 pounders was built. By this time numerous other batteries had been constructed in a great arc on the hills overlooking Seringapatam and the area between the batteries and the fortress had been completely cleared of enemy emplacements allowing trenches, which had their beginnings in Macintosh's ravine, to be extended right up to the banks of the Kaveri River, right beneath the city walls.

---

[86] *"Her Majesty's army, Indian and colonial forces : a descriptive account of the various regiments now comprising the Queen's forces in India and the colonies"* Canadian Institute for Historical Micro-reproductions

[87] A. Beatson *A View of the Conduct of the War with Tippoo Sultan* 1800

On the 2nd of May 1799 the British commenced heavy cannon fire on a North West section of Seringapatam's wall, directly in front of Macintosh's ravine, with the aim of creating a breach. Twenty nine 18 and 12 pound cannon fired continuously all through the daylight hours, either at the wall or at enemy gun emplacements which might be able to direct fire at the troops who would assault the intended breach in the wall. On the first day of this bombardment the artillery officer in command of the cannon fire from Macintosh's advance post, Lieutenant Colonel Montague, climbed up to the top of the battery's wall to inspect the damage being done to the fortress and was immediately hit by an enemy cannon ball that tore off his arm near the shoulder throwing him down on top of the men below. He died not long after.

By the 3rd of May 1799 the unrelenting bombardment of the British had created a wide breach in Seringapatam's wall however the cannon fire did not cease with the opening of the breach but continued on reducing the granite blocks to a slope of shattered rubble up which Macintosh and the other men in the storming party, would be able to scramble.

Before the first light of dawn on the 4th May Macintosh moved his battalion in with the other troops selected for the assault on breach in the advance trenches that terminated near the banks of the river below the battery. The storming troops numbered 2,494 Europeans and 1,882 Native Infantry plus their officers, including Lt. Macintosh and his 1st Battalion. The entire force was placed under the command of Major-General Baird who, determined to repay Tipu for the four years he had spent in the dungeons of Seringapatam, had specifically asked for the honour of leading the charge into the breach.

At precisely 1.30 pm on the 4th of May, exactly one month after the Madras Army had arrived at Seringapatam, General Baird, stepped out of the leading trench at the head of his troops

THE STORMING OF SERINGAPATAM: DEATH OF TIPPOO SAHIB.

Figure 18: Contemporary accounts rarely acknowledge the presence of the Native Infantry sepoys even though they represented more than 70% of the Company's army and were in the forefront of all the fighting. In this image from the *London Illustrated News* all the British forces are whites whereas, in reality, about 50% of the troops charging into the breech were Indian sepoys, not British soldiers.

and, waving his sword above his head, he called out:

> "Come my brave fellows, follow me and prove yourselves
> worthy of the name of British soldiers!"

With Baird in the lead Macintosh and the others sprang from the trenches and raced across the Kaveri River where they were exposed to withering cannon and musket fire from the city walls. Unfortunately the river waters had risen during the night due to heavy rains so the water which had been shallow the day before was now a deep and deadly current where "… men began to fall fast. All who were wounded inevitably drowned in a second ... plunged into an abyss fathoms deep."[88]

The details of the charge into the breach and the following battle were described in detail by another Scotsman, Lt. Rob Bayly, of H.M. 12th Regiment, who had been with Macintosh at Shawe's Post and who charged the breech alongside Macintosh.

"... After a month's continual fighting and hardships, a breach was reported practicable on the 3rd of May, and the following day was appointed for the storm. Towards evening the troops selected on this interesting occasion moved slowly down to the trenches, under the command of Baird. For nights and days had the troops suffered from excess of fatigue, up to their knees in water, and exposed to the fierce rays of the sun, fired at and rocketted from every direction, and subjected to continual alarms. We were, therefore, all rejoiced at the speedy prospect of a glorious termination to our incessant sufferings, advancing with all that animation and buoyant spirit so characteristic of British soldiers on the eve of a brilliant attack. At one o'clock p.m., on the 4th inst., Baird, taking out his watch, exclaimed: "The time has expired!" and leaped on the parapet of the trenches, exclaiming in a loud voice: "Now, my brave boys, follow me!" The enemy were at this moment quietly intent on their culinary preparations for dinner, and we experienced little loss, until we were floundering on the rocky bed of the river, when the men began to fall fast. All who were wounded were inevitably drowned in a second afterwards. One step the water scarcely covered the foot; the next we were plunged headlong into an abyss of fathoms deep. Thus scrambling over, the column at length reached the ascent of the breach, where numerous flankers who had preceded us were lying stretched on their backs, killed and wounded, some of the gallant officers waving their swords and cheering our men on. We dashed forward, and the top of the breach was soon crowned by our

---

[88] Lt. R Bayly (12th Regiment) *Description of the Assault on Seringapatam*

intrepid lads, and the British flag hoisted. But this was for a moment only. A sudden, sweeping fire from the inner wall came like a lightning blast, and exterminated the living mass. Others crowded from behind, and again the flag was planted. At this time General Baird was discovered on the ramparts. On observing a deep, dry, rocky ditch of sixty feet deep, and an inner wall covered with the troops of the enemy, he exclaimed: "Good God! I did not expect this!" His presence of mind did not desert him; he gave his directions in those cool, decided terms that a great man in the hour of danger and emergency knows so intuitively how to assume, and we were soon charging to the right and left of the breach along the ramparts of the outer wall. In the left attack, Tippoo was himself defending the traverses with the best and bravest of his troops. This impediment caused a sudden halt, but my gallant friend Woodhall impetuously rushed down a rugged confined pathway into the ditch, and ascended the second or inner wall, by an equally difficult road, mounted to the summit, followed by his company, the Light Infantry of the 12th. Ere he attained a footing, he had clasped a tuft of grass with his left hand, and was on the point of surmounting the difficulty, when a fierce Mussulman, with a curved, glittering scimitar, made a stroke at his head, which completely cut the bearskin from his helmet, without further injury Woodhall retaliated, separating the calf of the fellow's leg from the bone. He fell, and the gallant Light Bob was on the rampart in a moment, surrounded by a host of the enemy, whom, with the assistance of his company, he soon drove before him, thus relieving General Baird and his column on the outer wall from the destructive fire from the interior rampart, thereby saving hundreds of lives.

Tippoo finding his troops fired on from the inner ramparts, hastened to the Sallyport. Here Woodhall and his men were already in the interior of the town, prepared for the recontre, and a sharp firing ensued. The gateway was filled to the very top of the arch with dead and dying. The column under Baird had pursued the flying enemy to the Sallyport, and whilst Woodhall was bayoneting and firing in the front, they were also attacked in the rear. The body of Tippoo was afterwards amongst this promiscuous heap of slain. Neither Woodhall nor his men obtained a single article of plunder on the occasion, but a private of the 74th Regiment secured a very valuable armlet, which was sold to Doctor Mein of that corps for a few hundred rupees. It was ultimately discovered to be worth seventy or eighty thousand pounds. The doctor purchased the man's discharge, and settled him in Scotland on £100 pension per annum. The fortress now became one wild scene of plunder and confusion, but poor Woodhall and his men were appointed to extinguish the flames of some burning houses in the vicinity of the grand magazine of gunpowder, which, had it ignited, would have blown the whole garrison, friends and foes, into the air. He performed this arduous duty effectually, and although first in the town, his company were the only part of the regiment who did not reap any pecuniary reward for such daring heroism. The rest of the troops had filled their muskets, caps, and pockets with zechins, pagodas, rupees, and ingots of gold. One of our grenadiers, by name Platt, deposited in my hands, to the amount of fifteen hundred pounds' worth of the precious metals, which in six months afterwards he had dissipated in drinking, horse-racing, cock-fighting, and gambling ..."

After a short but intense battle the British cleared Tipu's troops from the ramparts with musket fire and bayonets after which the fighting moved into the maze of streets and allies of the city. Macintosh and his battalion fought their way through the streets until they found themselves outside Tipu's palace in the centre of the city. Here Macintosh was surprised to encounter the French colonel Louis Chappuis who, realising that the war was lost, surrendered himself to Macintosh and his Battalion. [89] Sporadic and sometimes fierce resistance continued in pockets around the city but the news that Tipu Sultan had been killed brought these to an end. By sunset all was quiet in Seringapatam.

Following the death of Tipu Sultan the East India Company reinstated Mysore's previous Hindu Wodeyar Dynasty by

---

[89] W. Richards *"Her Majesty's army, Indian and colonial forces : a descriptive account of the various regiments now comprising the Queen's forces in India and the colonies"*

installing one of the sons of the former Raja after which Mysore effectively became a British dependency.

Hugh Macintosh had distinguished himself throughout the campaign at Seringapatam and a year later, in August 1800, he was promoted to Captain and given full command of his battalion. (It is worth noting here that sometime around the end of 1801 a nineteen year old second lieutenant by the name of Henry Degraves was assigned to the 1st Battalion of the 8th Native Infantry under the command of Captain Macintosh. There can be no doubt that Henry Degraves and Hugh Macintosh soon became close friends, for six years later Henry's brother, Peter Degraves, married Macintosh's sister Sophia.)

With the new Raja installed in Seringapatam, Wellesley was made the commandant of the fortress and thereafter used it as a base from which he moved out to subdue any pockets of Indian resistance within the sphere of his concern; and where Wellesley went Captain Macintosh and his 1st Battalion also went, always in the forefront of Wellesley's battles, always victorious.

Once Mysore and its satellites had been subdued, and with the Company's position in Madras solid, Governor General Wellesley, Lord Mornington, focused his attention on the last native power that remained to challenge British dominance of India, the Marathas Confederation, which adjoined Mysore's northern borders.[90] In 1803 he launched a sustained campaign against them using the Madras Army under the command of his brother, now General Arthur Wellesley. In the Marathas campaign Wellesley fought many battles, two of which he later recalled were the fiercest and most challenging of his career and, as always, Macintosh and his men were there with him. These next battles that Macintosh fought in would cement Britain as the paramount power of India, put an end to Maratha

---

[90] R. Cooper *The Anglo-Maratha Campaigns and the Contest for India*

independence and, for General Wellesley, giving orders from the safety of a hillside overlooking the fighting, they would provide the experience that enabled him to defeat Napoleon at Waterloo. Wellesley's experience of these battles was very different from that of Hugh Macintosh who, led his troops into the thick of each battle and shared with them each moment of cannon and musket balls, spears, blood and fear with them. Always the possibility of a terrible death was just a breath away.

Toward Assaye

Captain Macintosh, Lieutenant Degraves and the 1st Battalion left Madras in February 1803 with the rest of the army to reach the territories of the Marathas, which lay well north of Mysore. It was a long march but as a captain in the Company's army Macintosh travelled in relative comfort with his own marquee and servants. This marquee, in which Macintosh dined with Henry Degraves and any of his other officers he chose to invite, was about 6 metres square (36 sq metres) with 2 metre high walls and a double fly sheet to keep out the dust and insects. At the end of a day's march his servants would have travelled ahead of the army to ensure that when Macintosh arrived at the night's camps site he would find his marquee erected and on entering see that his cot was already made up in case he wanted to have nap before the evening meal, which would be laid out for him on a table set with white linen and polished cutlery. This contrasted with the living arrangements of the European troops, who generally slept about 15 men to a tent, and the sepoys who, in the same sized tent, slept about 30 men.[91]

As well as a cook to prepare his meals Macintosh had a number of other Indian servants such as a butler, a boy to wait at his table and help him dress, another boy to clean his boots, shoes, knives etc, a groom and a grass cutter to provide feed for his horse.

---

[91] C. Blakiston *Twelve Years' Military Adventure* (London) 1829

His baggage and supplies as well as the supplies for his troops were carried in carts pulled by bullocks. As the commander of his battalion Macintosh was also responsible for organising and paying for the supplies required by the battalion as well as acquiring the beasts and drays to bring them.

Figure 19: Arthur Wellesley, later the Duke of Wellington, at the time he commanded Macintosh. Hugh Macintosh's battalion saved Wellesley from capture by Tipu Sultan. Thereafter they were known as "Wellesley's Battalion". Macintosh and his battalion accompanied General Wellesley, and led the charge, into every major battle that Wellesley commanded in India.

On the march across the Mysore plateau, the army was joined by troops from the various garrisons scattered across Mysore until the army numbered some 10,000 troops accompanied by an even greater number of servants and camp followers.

The camp followers included the families of the sepoys as well as merchants supplying everything a soldier might need; from food to prostitutes. As the campaign was expected to last at least six months, the army's official supplies followed the troops in a vast baggage train pulled by bullocks and camels. This vast mass moved in a straggling column across the Mysore plateau.

In his memoirs Captain Blakiston describes the camp that was set up at the end of each day's march and gives some insight into the size of the column Macintosh moved in. The camp was centred around General Wellesley's headquarters:

> On each flank of the headquarters, at some distance, the different departments of commissary, cattle agent, pioneers, engineers etc were encamped; and in the rear of the whole was the bazaar, generally extending in a line parallel to the front. When the ground permitted it the camp was formed in one straight line with a park for the artillery in the centre and the cavalry on one flank, the horses being picketed in straight lines or streets perpendicular to the front. The whole occupied the same space as the army would if drawn up in "line of battle" order.
>
> As the force encamped consisted of 10,000 men the front would be about 2 miles long and about half a mile deep; the greater part of this, not taken up by the regular tents of the army being covered with the booths of the bazaar and the small tents of the camp followers. Imagine over this space are scattered bipeds of every shade, from the most pale European to the darkest pariah of the lowest caste all intermingled with quadrupeds of every size from elephant, bullocks and camels down to goats, pigs and dogs.

Figure 20: Famine, due mainly to the constant warfare, was common during Macintosh's time in Mysore. The poor villagers, whose scant food reserves were seized by their overlords, bore the worst of things.

Riding at the head of his battalion as the army reached the borders of Mysore Macintosh passed through countryside that had been ravaged by years of war and famine; desolate villages of starving people who sat listlessly waiting to join the recently dead who lay on the ground beside them.

The Battle of Assaye took place on a field defined by the river Jouah and the village of Assaye. The British forces came upon their enemy unexpectedly after General Wellesley, acting on inaccurate intelligence, had split his force in two with the idea of entrapping the Marathas; instead the British found themselves facing Scindia's complete army, about 100,000 men, with only half their force or about 5,000 men. Scindia knew the route by which the British were approaching so the Marathas artillery, comprised of more than one hundred cannon manned by well trained troops, was positioned on a ridge overlooking the river and the flat ground above its banks. General Wellesley ordered four battalions of the Madras Native Infantry, flanked on both sides by Scottish Regiments, to charge directly at the enemy cannon. One of those battalions was the 1st Battalion of the 8th Regiment of Native Infantry, led by Captain Macintosh. Under heavy fire from the Marathas' guns on the ridge, Macintosh and Degraves, swords drawn, marched their battalion across the river and into range of the cannon. In ordered ranks they marched onto the field directly into the line of blazing enemy cannon where their ordered ranks were shattered by cannon balls and grapeshot. The scene was described graphically by Blakiston, who, mounted beside Wellesley, witnessed the action from a vantage point on the safe side of the river, out of the cannons' range.

> At this time the fire from the enemy's artillery became, indeed, most dreadful. In the space of less than a mile, 100 guns, worked with skill and rapidity, vomited forth death into our feeble ranks. It cannot, then, be a matter of surprise if, in many cases, the sepoys should have taken advantage of any irregularities in the ground to shelter themselves from the deadly shower, or even if, in some few instances, not all the endeavours of their officers could persuade them to move forward.[92]

Captain Macintosh, Lt. Degraves and the 1st Battalion were pinned down by the cannon; Macintosh was trying to move his troops forward as shrapnel and grapeshot sliced the air all around him. Degraves was hit by grapeshot and dropped to the ground clutching his shoulder. Macintosh ran to his friend and dragged him into the shelter of a small depression while around them the sepoys were being torn to pieces by cannon fire. Then, when it seemed that they must all perish, the Scottish troops charged in from the flanks to attack the ends of the line of

---

[92] C. Blakiston *Twelve Years' Military Adventure* (London) 1829 pp. 163-169

cannon with musket, bayonet and sword. As the Scots closed in on the Marathas' flanks there was a brief pause in the cannon fire.

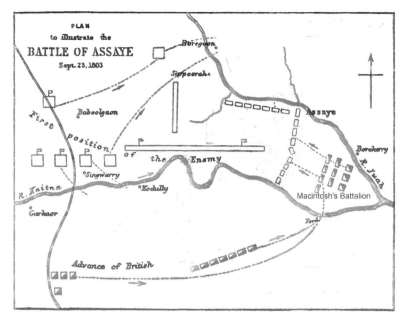

Figure 21: The Duke of Wellington later recalled the Battle of Assaye as being the most difficult battle of his career. Hugh Macintosh and his 1st Battalion led the charge at the Marathas cannon line across open ground. Lt. Henry Degraves was wounded in the charge at the cannon.

Macintosh left Degraves and rallied his battalion to take advantage of the distraction caused by the Scots. He rallied the sepoys into a firing line and sent a full volley, nearly 500 one ounce lead musket balls, crashing into the line of artillery directly in front of them. The 1st Battalion followed the volley with a bayonet charge, screaming their war cry as they raced at the line of cannon. The British bayonet charge was a fearful thing to face and many an enemy line broke before it however in this case the charge was met head on by the well trained Marathas infantry who emerged from their position behind the artillery line. With the Scots attacking the flanks and

Macintosh's troops attacking the centre, the battle quickly descended into a melee of British sword and bayonet against the Marathas' slashing broad-bladed spear and half pike. The Marathas fought with great courage, as Major Thorn described:

> "... (The Marathas) infantry stood till the English bayonets touched their breasts; the artillery men, with similar firmness, served their guns without receding an inch; and when they could no longer fire they used their tollwars, till they fell under the carriage wheels of their cannon; while the cavalry, in the same spirit, charged up to the very muzzles of our firelocks."

Below is a contemporary drawing of the charge of Macintosh's battalion at the Marathas artillery line; it shows clearly what it must have been like charging at a line of 100 firing cannon and the intensity of the hand to hand combat that followed.

Figure 22: A contemporary drawing of Macintosh and his sepoys charging the line of Marathas cannon, a charge which ultimately won the day for the British and spared Wellesley from a crushing defeat.

The tide of the bloody battle ebbed and flowed all day under the relentless tropical sun until, finally, the Marathas troops broke and fled, leaving their dead and wounded in the field. The wounded Marathas soon joined the dead, however, as Wellesley's troops walked around the battlefield and bayoneted the wounded where they lay. As a result the number of Marathas dead came to about 6,000 where as Wellesley lost 428 men killed and 1,138 wounded, or about one-third of his force. The surviving British soldiers were both exhausted and parched with thirst by the day-long battle beneath the blazing sun and the only readily available water was in the Jouah River, which Macintosh had crossed long hours earlier under blistering cannon fire. Now Macintosh and the other troops rushed to the same river to slake their thirst, as Captain Blakiston recalled:

> I shall never forget the rush to the river as soon as our safety would admit of the soldiers leaving their ranks; here, not withstanding that its scanty waters, from the number killed in crossing its bed, were completely tinged red with blood, yet few could resist the temptation to quench their burning thirst (in the bloody water).

Shocked by the extent of his defeat the Maratha prince Scindia soon made peace with the British however other Maratha nobles did not. The Raja of Berar was one of those who refused to surrender and, although deserted by his ally Prince Scindia, he continued to fight the British and engaged Wellesley again at the small fortified city of Argaum, reinforcing his local troops with a regiment of hardened Arab mercenaries. Once more Macintosh and his battalion led the charge into the fray and once more General Wellesley won the day.

From Argaum the Raja of Berar retreated to the most secure of his mountain forts, Gawilghur. Built on a mountain peninsular, its walls built on the edge of steep cliffs, Gawilghur was considered unassailable.

Gawilghur's defensive works consisted of two fortresses, one outer and one inner. Behind the wall of the Outer Fort was a deep ravine across which was the gate to the Inner Fort. An army could theoretically capture the Outer Fort before realizing that the greater task lay in assaulting the inner. The Inner Fort was protected by several gates, the first of which was the least defensible. After breaking through that first gate, however, an assaulting army would have to follow a narrow passage to a second gate, all the while being attacked by defenders from the walls above.

THE FORT OF GAWILGHUR—THE TOWER OVER THE PEER PUTTEH GATE.
From original drawing, Library East India House.

Figure 23: Perched on a rocky outcrop, surrounded by unclimbable cliffs, Gawilghur was considered impregnable and would have been so had it not been for the innovative bravery of a Scottish captain and his Highlanders.

This was largely the case when Arthur Wellesley's army attacked Gawilghur. Macintosh and the 1st Battalion, along with H.M. 11th Regiment of Foot succeeded in taking the Outer Fort after which they supported the attack on the inner fort while, at the same time, Highlanders diverted the attention of the defenders by false attacks from the south. It is likely that Macintosh would have met his death attacking the inner fort at Gawilghur had it not been for the bravery of another Scot, Captain Campbell, and his Light Company who discovered a way to climb the ravine and then scale wall above it, unseen, to gain access to the fortress and assault the gatehouses. While their comrades were attempting a futile assault on the immense main gate of the inner fort, being cut down by musket fire from the walls above, Campbell and his men fought their way through to the main gatehouse and opened the gate thereby allowing the soldiers being slaughtered in the narrow passage in front of the gate to access the fort and shelter.[93] Once inside the fortress the battle broke up into a series of skirmishes which the British quickly won.

The victory at Gawilghur largely brought an end to the Marathas resistance and to Macintosh's campaigning who, with his battalion, returned to Madras. Apart from the martial prestige that came with so many successes in battle the victories also brought financial benefits for Macintosh who, as a captain, was entitled to a share of the booty or 'prize money' seized from the various city-forts captured during the campaign.

Not long after his return to Madras, Captain Macintosh, now a veteran of two of the most important battles between the British and Indian forces, and many other smaller ones, applied for a

---

[93] For anyone interested in more details of Macintosh's exploits in India the first three books in Bernard Cornwell's *Sharpe* series follows the path of Macintosh through India almost exactly, beginning with *Sharpe's Tiger* and ending with *Sharpe's Fortress*.

furlough to return to England to see his friends and family. There can be no doubt that he must have been physically and emotionally exhausted by his years of war in India.[94]

---

[94] Part of the 1796 reforms introduced by the East India Company gave its Madras Army officers an entitlement to three years furlough after ten years of service. Three years off was not excessive given that the journey to England and then back to India would have taken upwards of a year at sea and that it would be another ten years before another furlough was granted, ten years that about only 20 % of officers would expect to survive.

Chapter Eight: Marriage and Mutiny

In 1804 Macintosh left India for the long and dangerous voyage back to England. Apart from the obvious reasons for taking furlough in England marriage was the other motive that would have turned Macintosh's mind to the motherland, for there was a chronic shortage of single European women in India. This shortage meant that any single woman of British or European descent who arrived in India was an extremely valuable commodity and far beyond the reach of a lowly captain such as Macintosh. Blakiston goes so far as to say that the shortage was such as to create a Madras "marriage market". In this "market" an attractive woman of pure European descent could expect to marry a high-ranked civil or military officer in the Company's service and thereby secure wealth and social status. He also added:

> "If of true European white, she is almost sure to go off tolerably well; but no (female) mixture of the Asiatic will suit persons of any rank."

Such was the demand and the structure of Madras' European society that Macintosh would have had little or no chance of getting himself a European bride there. Conversely the idea of marrying a woman of mixed or Asian descent was tantamount to social suicide in the prejudiced expatriate society of 19th century Madras. To get a wife Macintosh needed to return to Britain.

While we know very little of Macintosh's parents we do know that his mother and sister Sophia were in London and that Sophia would certainly have accompanied her brother as he fulfilled the important duty expected of officers returning to home, that of delivering letters and messages to the family of their closest friends, the brother officers who still remained in India. One of Macintosh's closest friends was Lieutenant Henry

Degraves (who would not be entitled to furlough until at least 1809), whose mother and aunt lived together in London. Macintosh would have arrived at Mrs Degraves' home with a bundle of letters and exotic gifts from her son. He would have been invited to stay the evening and dine with the Degraves family and to give them news of their soldier son; as well as his own news and views of the situation in India. There can be no doubt that Mrs Degraves and her extended family would have sat transfixed around the dinner table listening to Captain Macintosh's tales of terrible battles and exotic locations. It was a meeting that would ultimately result in two marriages, for it is likely that this is when Sophia Macintosh met Peter Degraves.

Amongst those gathered at Mrs Degraves' home to meet Captain Macintosh would have been her neighbours and close friends, the family of William and Catherine Nicholson. William Nicholson was an eminent English scientist famous for being the first person to use electricity to separate water into its component elements of hydrogen and oxygen. Nicholson would have particularly enjoyed talking to Macintosh as he himself had worked for the East India Company in his youth and had made two trips to India. The Nicholson's eldest unmarried daughter was Mary, an interesting and adventurous young woman of about twenty, who would soon become Hugh Macintosh's wife. Although little is known of the early life of Mary Nicholson much may be inferred by a brief examination of the unusual influences and people who surrounded her from her birth in London in November 1787 until she moved to India in early 1807.[95]

Prior to her marriage to Macintosh, Mary Nicholson lived with her family in Red Lion Square in Soho during the same period that Henry Degraves also lived there and there can be little doubt that she would have known the Degraves family well.

---

[95] Register of Baptisms Church of St Marylebone 1787 London

112

Certainly Peter Degraves knew the Nicholson family, for he later claimed (falsely) to have been head assistant to William Nicholson in his laboratory. Mary Nicholson grew up surrounded by many of the foremost thinkers of her time; friends and colleagues of her father who was also a respected philosopher, writer, publisher, engineer and inventor and member of the Coffee House Philosophical Society. His close associates included James Watt, Joseph Priestly and William Boulton the founder of the Soho Mint where, fourteen years later, the Macintosh and Degraves silver shilling would be made. William Nicholson's closest friend was philosopher and writer, William Godwin, whose only daughter later became Mary Shelley, the author of *Frankenstein*.

Figure 24: Renowned British physicist and philosopher, William Nicholson, was the first man to separate water into Hydrogen and Oxygen. Nicholson was a mentor of Mary Shelley and he is acknowledged as the inspiration for her novel *Frankenstein*.

Godwin's wife, Mary Wollstonecraft, was an early radical feminist and philosopher who wrote, amongst other works, *A Vindication of the Rights of Women*. After the difficult birth of her daughter Wollstonecraft fell seriously ill and was nursed around the clock by Nicholson and his family up until the moment of her death in 1797. Mary Nicholson was about ten years old when Mary Wollstonecraft died and so for all her early life the future Mrs Macintosh would have had close connections with the thoughts and philosophies of this forward-thinking woman. There can also be little doubt that Macintosh's future wife was like a big sister to the young Mary (Godwin) Shelley as it is widely acknowledged that it was Mary Shelley's close connection to William Nicholson that gave her the understanding of biology and electricity that was to be the inspiration for *Frankenstein*. Another clue to Mary Nicholson's nature is the simple fact that she was prepared to marry Hugh Macintosh and move with him to live in India, for such a move was a rare and radical one for a well bred woman of her time.

Of significant influence on her decision would have been the fact that her father had, as a young man, made two trips to India. William Nicholson, who was fluent in French and Italian, was also responsible for translating several travel commentaries, including the *Memoirs and Travels of Mauritius Augustus Count de Benyowsky* (2 vols., 1789); so there can be little doubt that he would have told his children tales of his travels to India, filling their minds with exotic imaginings. Another factor which would have influenced Mary's decision to marry Macintosh was that the casualties that resulted from the war with Napoleon had caused a general shortage of marriageable men in England. This would undoubtedly have made an unmarried, well-educated officer, 30 years of age, with a career in the East India Company's army an attractive proposition. There would also have been some subtle pressure on her to marry from her family as her father, whilst prolifically productive in his various endeavours, was not able to turn his technical and scientific achievements to a financial advantage. In other words, William Nicholson was, as they said in the early 19th century, "financially embarrassed" and was destined to die a virtual pauper less than ten years later.

On the 31st October 1806 Captain Macintosh married Mary Nicholson and shortly after they set sail for Madras. The newly weds would have had a private cabin on one of the Company's East Indiamen and during the six-month ocean voyage their first and only son, William Hugh Macintosh, was conceived.

Figure 25: Mary Wollstonecraft, an early radical feminist, was a close family friend and influence on Macintosh's future wife, Mary Nicholson.

Once back in Madras, Macintosh and his wife would have spent some weeks performing the necessary social and official engagements before travelling through Mysore to the hill fort of Chittaldroog where Macintosh was to take command of the garrison.[96]

The town's garrison was comprised of his own 1st Battalion of the 8th Regiment and an artillery battalion from the 15th Regiment of the Madras Native Infantry.

Before he left Madras, conscious of his new responsibilities as a family man and knowing the high mortality rate of men in his profession, Macintosh took out an insurance policy against his death or serious injury with the recently created Madras Military Fund, a pension fund set up to provide for the many widows and children of officers of the Madras Army.

Figure 26: An 1803 painting of the fortress city of Chittaldroog, where Macintosh was the Commandant, and which was his and Mary Macintosh's first home in India. Backed up against the mountains and encircled by stone walls the fortress was considered impregnable.

---

[96] Anglicised to Chitteldrug in Macintosh's time and is now called Chitradurga.

Macintosh's heavily pregnant wife would have travelled by a slow but comfortable cart, with Macintosh riding along side and a full entourage of servants to make the journey as comfortable as possible. Chittaldroog was strategically situated in the central highlands of Mysore between Seringapatam and Bangalore and was considered to be almost impregnable because of its location at the base of a range of steep and rugged hills. With this natural barrier at its back all approaches to the town were protected by stone walls built in such a way as to gain the maximum advantage from the rugged environment. As the commandant of this extensive fort Macintosh would have had one of the most prestigious residences there with a bevy of servants. Unfortunately, whilst exotic and secure, Chittaldroog had a reputation for being an unhealthy place to live because of a lack of clean water. During the rainy season water was caught and stored in reservoirs built in the rocky hills above the fort; however this water soon became stagnant and rank once the rains had passed and the long, hot dry season began. As a consequence many water borne diseases, including cholera, were endemic.

Sadly Mary Macintosh shared the fate of her namesake, Mary Wollstonecraft, and that of many other 19th century women. Their son William Hugh Macintosh, was born on 27th December 1807, Mary Macintosh died not long after.

After the death of his wife, Macintosh remained at Chittaldroog as the commandant. It is likely he planned to keep his son with him until the boy reached the age of seven or eight, at which time an officer's son would have been expected to attend a boarding school in Madras or back in England.

An interesting story comes down to us from Macintosh's time as commandant of Chittaldroog, through the memoirs of Peter Degraves' grand-daughter, Ada Wilson. This story tells a lot of Macintosh the man.

Generally the British tended not to interfere with Indian traditional life however on one occasion Macintosh heard of a young girl, who had been married as a child to a young boy. The boy, her husband, had died and was being cremated. Macintosh arrived on the scene of the cremation just as the boy's relatives were about to ceremonially throw his child bride into the funeral pyre in the act known as *sati* (or suttee). Traditionally Hindu widows were expected to commit *sati* as a gesture of respect and love for their dead husband and because of the belief that it removed any sins that the husband had committed, making him able to have a happy afterlife. This was supposed to be voluntary for the widow, but, should the women not wish to burn themselves alive, they were often forced to commit *sati* by the family of their husband.

Macintosh broke up the ceremony and rescued the young girl from the flames and her hostile in-laws. Now however, the girl, though obviously greatly relieved at not being burned, was a social outcaste with nowhere to go, her husband's family would kill her and her own parents would not risk the shame of bringing her back into their home. She begged Macintosh to accept her as his slave, which he did in order that she would have somewhere safe to live. The Degraves' family tradition has it that he later sent her to be educated at a convent school and supported her until she reached adulthood.

Less than two years after the birth of his son and not long after he had saved the girl from *sati* bad luck again intervened in Macintosh's life when he became, inadvertently, involved in the mutiny of the officers of the Madras Army against the governor of Madras, an event known as the "White Mutiny".

The 1809 "White Mutiny" had its roots in changes made to the conditions of employment for the Company's army which were introduced as a result of its general reorganisation in 1796. Amongst other things, these changes removed, or attempted to remove, various official and unofficial "fringe benefits" which the Company's army officers had come to think of as their just entitlements. The changes also had the unexpected effect of limiting the officers' opportunities for promotion by gradually but significantly increasing the numbers of junior officers in the ranks. The discontent grew over the years and, whilst the Company made some concessions to accommodate the officers' demands, serious issues remained unresolved. Foremost amongst these was the fact that the allowances for housing and other living expenses were significantly greater for Company officers in Bengal than in Madras, despite the fact that the cost of living was higher in Madras. This and other perceived differences in the way they were treated placed the Madras officers under greater financial hardship than their Bengal counterparts, and caused them to feel less valued by the Company.

Another issue, which affected Macintosh directly, was a considerable reduction to an allowance called "off-reckoning" which was a bonus officers, such as Macintosh, enjoyed if they made savings on clothing and equipping their troops. This had the effect of further reducing the income of the Madras officers whilst further increasing the differences between them and the Bengali officers.

Another issue of contention was the abolition by the Company of the Bazaar Tax, a long-held (though unofficial) right— inherited from minor local-government functionaries of the various Indian regimes when they were replaced by British officers—of the officer commanding a fort, a cantonment or such, to levy a tax on the stall holders and shop owners in bazaars in their precinct. The Bazaar Tax enabled officers to accumulate capital against their retirement at a time when there were no pension funds.[97] Despite the later introduction of a pension, the officers were extremely reluctant to surrender a tax which provided an immediate financial benefit in exchange for a pension that they might receive in the distant future if they were lucky enough to live that long, which was a genuine concern as only one in seven officers actually lived long enough to receive their pension.

Thrown into this conglomeration of complaints, the Madras officers also had a longstanding jealousy of the officers of the King's army. This problem originated in an 18th century rule that gave any officer of the King's army automatic seniority over any officer of the Company's army. This rule meant that a junior Captain of a couple of years' standing in the King's Army would outrank a senior Major or Colonel of twenty or thirty years' standing in the Company's Army. There was also a perception that officers from the King's Army were being given preferential treatment in appointments to the best and most lucrative commands or staff positions.

The Company's officers were also aware that, as a direct result of their efforts in subduing Central and Southern India, more and more regions saw military rule being replaced by the civilian rule of magistrates and other administrators whose salaries were often twice as large as those of the army officers whose functions they acquired.

Added to this simmering cauldron of discontent were the growing number of junior officers whose ranks had been deliberately swollen by the Company in an attempt to increase the numbers of British-born officers who, it was felt, were more reliable than the Indian-born officers of British descent. These

---

[97] Although the Bazaar Tax was officially abolished after the 1796 re-organisation when a pension plan was introduced by the Company quite a number of officers continued to collect it.

young men had arrived in India with hopes of fortune and glory only to find that the once-legendary opportunities for personal advancement were fast disappearing, if not already gone.

In the background, adding subtle heat to the discontent in the Madras Army, were the influences of the more liberal thinking members of society that found expression in Britain through the Whig party. The Whigs had a significant number of supporters in Madras, amongst whom were a Supreme Court judge, Sir Henry Gwillim; a leading barrister, Charles Marsh; and a successful free-trader named Thomas Parry, all of whom were agitating for changes to the Company's monopoly and powers.

In 1807, well aware of the fermenting discontent in Madras, Sir George Barlow took up his appointment as Governor of the Madras Presidency. It was a step down for Barlow for he had recently held the post of Governor General of all of India, being promoted into that position after the sudden death of Governor General Lord Cornwallis in October 1805, who was serving a second term in India.

Barlow had very definite views on the nature and use of authority, that did not include compromise of consultation, and he moved rapidly to quell the drift toward rebellion amongst the Company's officers. It is not within the scope of this work to examine Barlow's actions and their consequences except in the context of their effects on Hugh Macintosh. It is sufficient to say that, when in 1809, the disgruntled officers presented a list of demands to the government; Barlow refused to meet them and instead countered with a list of threats. Most of these officers had been involved in the vicious fighting of the Mysore and Marathas campaigns and had seen many of their fellows die in the Company's service. They felt that the Company was not rewarding them for the sacrifices they had made in its service.

After a protracted period of posturing from both sides, in May 1809 the officers broke into open revolt. The mutiny was not a tightly co-ordinated action and took different forms in different areas, as would be expected with such a widely scattered group of officers commanding garrisons all across southern India, who could only communicate by letters that often took several days to reach their destinations.

This meant that each group of mutineers had to make decisions based on information that was often a week or more old.

The mutiny at the fortress at Seringapatam began in August under the leadership of Lt. Colonel Bell of the Madras Artillery who took control of the fort and seized the Company's armoury, treasury and granary. The mutineers then expelled the Company's civilian officials and indicated that they would fight to the death rather than surrender on the terms demanded by Governor Barlow. Once he had secured Seringapatam Lt. Colonel Bell sent out letters to the commandants of surrounding forts and asked them to come and join him at Seringapatam where, he said, there were sufficient supplies to withstand a major siege and the money with which to pay the wages of the sepoy troops, thereby ensuring their loyalty. To further make certain that they had sufficient funds to finance their rebellion Bell also seized a passing Company caravan that was carrying a treasure of 30,000 pagodas (about £12,000 or enough cash to pay the wages of two thousand sepoys for six months).[98]

Macintosh, the commandant at Chittaldroog, was among those who received Bell's invitation and the assurance from Bell that he and his brother officers were prepared to fight to the death against the oppressive demands of Governor Barlow.

---

[98] The pagoda was the official currency of Madras until 1818; a gold coin worth around half a pound sterling. M. Edney *Mapping an Empire: the geographical construction of British India* 1990 p.17

Figure 27: Sir George Barlow was a man who had no doubt of his right to rule or his authority. A strict disciplinarian he was not interested in negotiating with officers who he considered to be his social inferiors.

Macintosh responded in the affirmative, no doubt being moved by a sense of loyalty to his brother officers as well as by considerations of what the loss of the Bazaar Tax and other incidental sources of income meant. On the morning of the 10th August, he and the other officers (including Lieutenant Henry Degraves) and the two battalions garrisoned at Chittaldroog —a total of about 1120 officers and men plus the families of the sepoys and other camp followers—marched out of the fort and headed for Seringapatam.

Unfortunately for Macintosh the government forces in Bangalore had received word of his intentions and despatched a significant force, including the feared 59th Dragoons belonging to His Majesty's army, a detachment of light infantry and a large number of Mysore cavalry, to prevent Macintosh and his men from reaching Seringapatam.

The Mysore cavalry technically belonged to the Raja and were under the command of an Indian officer named Rama Row. The government realised that the Mysore horse would be the first to reach Macintosh, and Rama Row was under orders to treat with him under a flag of truce and to try to convince him to halt his march until negotiations could be undertaken that might resolve the issue. The two men met only a day's march out from Seringapatam and Macintosh invited Rama Row to share tea with him in his tent where, after extended discussions Macintosh assured Rama Row that he was determined not to be the first to commence hostilities and, on that basis, he agreed to a temporary halt. Unfortunately, the following evening Macintosh received another letter from Bell at Seringapatam urging him to make haste as the fort was under threat of imminent attack. Macintosh's response was to mobilise his men and, at ten o'clock that night, they began a forced march toward Seringapatam. Seeing this, Rama Row attacked the Chittaldroog troops with his cavalry but was easily repulsed by Macintosh's seasoned infantry. However at dawn H.M. army's mounted Dragoons joined with the Mysore Horse and the combined force rapidly closed on Macintosh's forces. First catching up with the camp followers with their carts, animals and children straggling some way behind the ranks of marching troops; the Dragoons and Mysore Horse "… commenced a most inhuman butchery … they did not spare even women and children …".

Figure 28: To save his sepoys and their families Macintosh was forced to turn and fight the feared Dragoons as well as the Mysore horse. Severely outnumbered Macintosh was almost beheaded by a slashing sabre.

The mounted soldiers slammed into the unarmed civilians, using sabre and spear to tear through them as they tried to run to the safety of Seringapatam, which was now only about three kilometres away.[99]

Seeing the slaughter of the camp followers, including the wives and children of his sepoys, on the same ground where he had risked his life for the East India Company to fight the forces of Tipu Sultan ten years earlier, Macintosh was now forced to turn and fight against the King's Army or allow them to slaughter his people unhindered. It was a decision that must have torn Macintosh between his allegiance to King and Country and his loyalty to his troops and "brother officers".

---

[99] Cardew *The White Mutiny* Letter of James Baker to his brother; August

To give the bulk of his troops and their families a chance to reach Seringapatam, Macintosh led a small force out to counterattack the marauding horsemen while Henry Degraves led the remainder of their people to safety. However before the two men parted Henry Degraves brought his horse up beside Macintosh and insisted that they swap caps for Degraves' cap was a sturdier one than the cap Macintosh was wearing; it had a thick leather flap of four layers of camel hide that hung down to cover and protect the wearer's neck. Degraves, seeing the Dragoons charging toward them, sabres drawn, insisted that Macintosh take his cap and Macintosh did.

As Degraves and the bulk of the Chittaldroog garrison raced toward Seringapatam Macintosh formed his troops into battle lines to block the charging cavalry. In the fight that followed Macintosh received a sabre slash to his neck which knocked him off his horse and cut through the thick camel hide flap that was protecting his neck, as well as through the silk neck scarf beneath the leather. Fortunately by the time the sword blade reached his actual neck its force was all but spent so he suffered only a minor wound rather than the intended decapitation.

Under the protective cover of cannon fire from the walls of Seringapatam, Henry Degraves and the battalion's remaining officers managed to get about 700 of the Chittaldroog troops to safety, though they had no choice but to leave Macintosh lying in the dust, stunned and wounded. The Dragoons abandoned their pursuit of the fleeing troops and turned on what remained of Macintosh's rear guard, chasing down and killing the fleeing Sepoys and capturing their commander. Of the men who had stayed with Macintosh in the rear guard action, including another British officer, almost all were killed or wounded. Macintosh, being both an officer and British, was taken as a prisoner to the authorities in Mysore; it was the end of his career in India.

Not long after Macintosh's capture, the mutiny was brought to a negotiated end by the sensible intervention of the new Governor General of India, Lord Minto. Under the terms of settlement between Minto and the mutineers, all officers would be reinstated without penalty except where they had been directly involved in the spilling of the blood of loyal forces. Only a handful of officers fell into this category; Macintosh was one of them. Lieutenant Degraves was pardoned, it being argued that he had not taken part in the battle with the Dragoons and in any case that he had been obeying Macintosh's orders. At his Court Marshall in early 1810, Macintosh was found guilty of mutiny, for which the penalty was death. However, not wanting to aggravate an already delicate situation with the Company's officers, Lord Minto did not press for capital punishment. Of all the officers who took part in the mutiny, only Macintosh and three others were dishonourably discharged from the East India Company's Army and banned from future service.[100] It was a mild punishment for such a serious offence, but for Macintosh it carried serious consequences, including the loss of his pension and the end of his career.

---

[100] A. Cardew *The White Mutiny* (Bombay) 1929 pp. 136-140

Figure 29: A formal painting of the Crown Prince Abbas Mirza who promoted Macintosh to the rank of General in the Persian army.

Although Macintosh was in a very difficult position—convicted of mutiny and dishonourably discharged from the Company's army—he still had the sympathy and respect of the army's officers who knew that he had been both true to their united cause and fought bravely and honourably to protect his troops. Though he could well be described as a most honourable mutineer, and while most of the instigators of the mutiny escaped all sanctions, Macintosh had to pay a high price for the stand he took and decision he made to defend his people at Seringapatam. He had lived in India almost exclusively since he was 16 years old; his only child had been born in India and his wife had died there: he knew no other life.

Macintosh was officially dismissed from the Madras Army in April 1810. Fortunately, his reputation, personal and family connections ensured that he did not end up destitute, for there were opportunities for well educated men with Macintosh's language skills and military background. However, these would not be in India, where the Company's control was now almost absolute. Perhaps in preparation for the long and dangerous sea journey back to England, Macintosh had his son, William Hugh Macintosh (aged two years and seven months), baptised at the chapel of Fort St George in July 1810.

As Macintosh and young William were sailing back to England, his old school friend from Harrow, Henry Ellis, was establishing his presence in the Shah's court in Tehran, a fact which was to have the most profound implications for Macintosh.

Unable to inherit his father Lord Hobart's title because of his illegitimacy, Ellis had, never-the-less, used his brilliant mind and family influence to make a successful career as a diplomat in Asia. Henry Ellis and Macintosh had remained in contact over the years particularly when Ellis was working for the East India Company in a civilian capacity in Bengal. Unlike Macintosh, Henry Ellis had continued his formal education and, like

Macintosh, he had also become an expert in Asian languages, including Persian. Ellis had also used his social connections with his natural talents in language and related areas to advance himself as a diplomat. At the time Macintosh was Commandant of Chitaldroog and became involved in the Madras mutiny, in 1809, Ellis was travelling to Persia with Sir John Malcolm on a diplomatic mission aimed at reducing French influence in the court of the Shah. Then two years later, not long after Macintosh's court marshal, Ellis again travelled to Persia attached to Sir Gore Ouseley's Embassy to the Court of the Shah of Persia in the capacity of a secretary.

It seems likely that Ellis joined the party of Ouseley, the newly appointed British Ambassador to Persian, at Bombay in January 1811, when Ouseley's ship, the *Lion*, stopped to pick up additional supplies, guides and a significant number of British military officers who were to be advisors and trainers to the Persian army. [101] Whilst there had been several diplomatic missions sent from Britain to Tehran over the preceding decades, Ouseley was the first British Ambassador appointed to Persia in over 150 years. One of his primary aims in travelling to Tehran was related to training Persian troops in European-style warfare to prevent Russian or French penetration of North India via the land route from Europe. [102]

For its part Persia was seeking to capitalise on the fact that the European powers were vying for influence and alliances with

---

[101] W. Ouseley *Travels in Various Counties of the East, More Particularly Persia*

[102] The reasons for Sir Gore's embassy were multiple. At the time of Ousleley's embassy Britain was at war with both Russia and France. The French had held considerable influence in Tehran through the first decade of the 19th century but that influence was on the wain and Ouseley was expected to make a definitive alliance with Persia against France. The East India Company was also concerned about the possibility of the Afghans invading northern India and saw Persia as a means of controlling Afghanistan.

the major powers in Asia, and thereby modernise its armies in response to Russian aggression at its northern borders. For most of the first decade of the 19th century the French had held sway in Tehran with promises of military assistance. However, by 1809 the Shah's advisors realised that the French would not or could not fulfil their promises. This gave the British a diplomatic opportunity which they quickly seized.

One of Ouseley's offerings to the Shah that would ultimately involve Macintosh was to provide experienced high ranking British officers as military advisers to train the Persian troops in modern British methods of warfare.[103] These British soldiers were almost immediately involved in heavy action against the Russians in 1812 when Persia and Russia engaged in full-scale war. However, while Ouseley's mission was still in progress, Britain and Russia made peace, part of the terms of this peace was that Britain would no longer supply military support to Persia. As a result Ouseley received orders to ensure all British officers ceased their work within the Persian Army. There is no doubt that this would have placed Ouseley in an awkward position at the Shah's court had he not been able to exploit a loophole in the Anglo/Russian treaty. This entailed the covert recruitment of ex-British officers into the Persian Army and in late 1812, two former officers, Christie and Lindsay, commanded sections of the Persian Army against the Russians in the decisive Battle of Aslanduz. However, for the long term there was probably no one better suited for such a role than Hugh Macintosh, who was both a highly experienced military commander and also fluent in the Persian language.

---

[103] The superiority of European military tactics had been effectively demonstrated in India for more than half a century, as had the hiring of European officers to train native forces. Hyder Ali, Tipu and the Marathas ruler Mahadji Sindhia, to name just a few, had done so with great effect, mostly using French officers.

In 1813 Henry Ellis returned to England, located Macintosh who was probably staying with his mother in London, and offered him a position that saw him nominally attached to the British Embassy. It was a perfect opportunity for Hugh Macintosh, his son William had just reached the age when boys from his social strata were sent to boarding school; certainly it was at about the same age that Macintosh was sent to Harrow. Macintosh's mother was still alive so William had his paternal grandmother and both of his maternal grandparents all living in London (William Macintosh's grandfather, William Nicholson, died in 1815 while his two grandmothers lived at least until the 1830's.). All this meant that Macintosh could safely leave his son in England in the care of close relatives while he pursued his career, and fortune, in Persia.

Whilst Macintosh technically went to Persia as part of a British diplomatic mission he was actually in the employ of the Shah but assigned to the Shah's son Abbas Mirza, who was the effective 'commander in chief' of the Persian armed forces.

Either the Shah or the Crown Prince gave Macintosh the rank of a General in the Persian army and an excellent remuneration package. Whilst there is no exact figure on Macintosh's salary, Sir John Malcolm (a regular British envoy to Persia over many years) stated that the Shah, to encourage Persian soldiers and officers to participate in the European training programs, offered pay "... superior to any other class in Persia" as well as excellent fringe benefits that included land grants. Persian officers under the leadership of the European trainers were being paid up to five hundred Tomans (only slightly less than £500) per annum. This amount was slightly more than wage of an East India Company Colonel, so it is reasonable to assume that Macintosh, with the rank of General, would have been paid considerably more than that.

Apart from training and commanding Persian troops, Macintosh was also asked to translate British army "rules and regulations" into Persian to enable Persian officers to follow British command procedures. Toward the end of 1813, Macintosh set out on the overland route to Tehran in a party of diplomats and former officers led by the new British *chargé d'affaires* Henry Willock, who had also served in the East India Company's Madras Army.

Willock had travelled to Persia several times from India and was an acknowledged expert on both the language and the culture. Ten years Macintosh's junior Willock would have been well aware of the older officer's military reputation and exploits as he had been stationed in Madras at the same time as Macintosh. The route the party travelled was first by ship, over the Mediterranean, to a port in Palestine then, on horseback, overland to Tehran.

Figure 30: Persian soldier from the time Macintosh was in Persia.

Once in Persia Macintosh appears to have acted in various capacities for the British Embassy and for the Shah before being made Commandant of the large frontier city of Erivan where, as well a organising the Shah's troops he advised the city's governor, Hosein Khan, on tactics to thwart the continual Russian encroachments on Erivan. The family of Hosein Khan was highly favoured by the Shah and the Crown Prince and as such was second in power only to the Shah's family.

Figure 31: The Hall of Mirrors: palace of Hosein Khan at Erivan where Macintosh, as Commandant, met with the Shah's most trusted governor and advised him on military tactics and strategies. Hosein Khan was also a close friend of the Crown Prince so it is certain that all three men would have met and dined together in this fabulous palace.

Interestingly the position Macintosh held in Erivan was similar to that he had held in Chittaldroog although now, instead of the

East India Company bureaucrats, he was under the direct command of the Persian Crown Prince, Abbas Mirza, with whom he developed a close, long lasting, friendship.

Figure 32: Crown Prince of Persia: Abbas Mirza (1789-1833)

Abbas Mirza, whilst renowned for his valour in battle, was also a well educated reformer who attempted to modernise Persian society with a program that included sponsoring many young Persian students to travel to and study in Europe.

Abbas Mirza's attempts to modernise Persia were fiercely resisted by the many conservative elements within the Royal Court of his father the Shah. These reactionary conservatives were probably responsible for his premature death in October 1833 aged 44, which was officially declared to be death from a disease of the liver, but was more likely to have been from poison administered over a long period by his rivals.

Russia and Persia had been at war, on and off, for many years however a treaty, known as *The Treaty of Gulistan,* negotiated in October 1813, brought overt hostilities between Persia and Russia to an end. However despite the treaty, which placed onerous conditions of Persia, tensions continued and border issues were sensitive as military activities continued. [104] Erivan became a frontier post and its strength and readiness against possible Russian aggression was critical to Persia's future security. At the same time the destabilisation caused by Persia's military losses to Russia inspired uprisings against the Shah in various quarters of Persia, which Abbas Mirza and Macintosh were regularly sent to quell. It was during one of these sorties, sometime toward the end of 1818 or early in 1819, that Macintosh was severely wounded, the exact nature of his wounds is not known but they were bad enough to bring a permanent end to his military career and to his years in Persia.[105]

---

[104] During this period Henry Ellis returned to Persia as the deputy Ambassador *ad interim* through 1814 and 1815 primarily to finalise the treaty between Persia and Britain. Macintosh would later use Ellis as a character referee when he applied to Lord Bathurst for permission to immigrate to Hobart in 1821.

[105] These wounds were mentioned by Edward Markham, who met Macintosh at the Cascades in Hobart in 1834. Markham stated in his publication *Voyage to Van Dieman's Land,* that Macintosh spent many years in Persia teaching the Persians "European tactics" and also that he was "severely wounded".

At this point, wounded and unable to continue an active military career Macintosh's preference was to return to India, where he had spent almost all his adult life, however to do so he needed to be 'forgiven' by the East India Company and have the exile imposed at his court martial lifted. Abbas Mirza wrote personally to the East India Company's Court of Directors to plead his friend's case and to ask for his reinstatement in the Madras Army, or some similar position. The Court of Directors politely refused the Crown Prince's request so, with the promise of a pension from the Shah, Macintosh left Persia in 1819 and returned to Britain where he renewed his acquaintance with his brother-in-law Peter Degraves. This was an acquaintance that the virtually penniless Degraves would have immediately seen as being something that he might turn to his advantage, for Macintosh had returned with a considerable amount of capital accumulated over his years in India and Persia, a sum in excess of £10,000. Combined with the pension that had had been promised from treasury of the Shah of Persia this placed Hugh Macintosh in a relatively solid financial position.

Macintosh's return to England occurred about the same time that Degraves was attempting to convince the Stewart-Mackenzies to back his various proposals for the Isle of Lewis. When Degraves realised that Stewart-Mackenzie was not going to help facilitate his great works on Lewis, he reverted to his "Plan B", which involved buying a ship and sailing to Hobart to build a saw mill. As with the other schemes Degraves attempted to initiate, he lacked cash. Whilst he had the ideas, expertise and energy, he had no capital to buy a ship or all the other things necessary for such a vast undertaking: however, his brother-in-law did. It was an interesting situation, for it is likely that Macintosh was at a loss with what to do with himself now that his military career was finally over. He was one of many out-of-work military officers scattered across Britain as a result of the end of the Napoleonic Wars and the submission of India and though he had the advantage of possessing significant capital it was not a large enough sum to provide him with an income adequate to support himself and his son. Macintosh would have known of men in a similar position to himself making the choice of immigrating to Australia. The astute Degraves would have been aware of all this and it would not have taken much "grooming" from Degraves to paint Macintosh a promising picture of a new life in Hobart where Degraves could use his genius to create a huge income for them both with the help of Macintosh's capital. Degraves' argument would have been greatly assisted by the fact that in this same period the idea of emigrating to Australia was very popular in Scotland, particularly for men in Macintosh's situation, with the local press and various prominent figures promoting the benefits of such emigration.[106]

If Macintosh was open to his brother-in-law's ideas he was also no fool. He knew that if he was going to supply the bulk of the capital then he should be the major partner in the venture, which is one of the reasons why in late 1820, when they purchased the *Hope,* the ownership of the vessel remained solely the name of Macintosh.

---

[106] D.S. MacMillan, *Scotland and Australia 1788-1850* (Oxford) 1967

Section Three: The *Hope* and on to Hobart.

Chapter Ten: The History of the Colonial Ship *Hope*.

Figure 33: Built about 1790 the *Hope* was a "sharp built" ship, a precursor to the "clipper", its hull was designed for speed, sacrificing carrying capacity.

There are many versions of Degraves' life during the period from 1821 to 1824. All of these, however, revolve around the ship *Hope* and it is important to understand the history of that vessel in order to unpick the tangled web of claim, counter claim and deliberate deception.

The *Hope* is primarily remembered because in 1823-24 she carried Macintosh and Degraves from England to Van Diemen's Land, along with the personnel, machinery and other equipment that they would use to build their sawmill at the Cascades on the slopes of Mount Wellington.[107] The *Hope* is also remembered because of her connection with a famous Tasmanian legend generally known as the lost treasure of Bruny Island. This popular story has its source in the vessel's loss on Hope Beach on South Arm at the mouth of the Derwent River in April 1827.[108]

When Macintosh purchased the *Hope* she was already an old ship with a long history—a history that Degraves later deliberately obscured. Consequently there is much more to the story of this vessel than is told by the many maritime history books within which she is mentioned in the context of being Degraves' ship. For apart from the brief period she was an instrument of Degraves' schemes, but still during the period that Macintosh was her actual owner, she continued her role as a British colonial ship, carrying whale oil, whale bone and seal skins as well as timber and other agricultural produce from Hobart back to England or along the circuitous Australasian trading route. On the return route from England the *Hope* carried migrant passengers as well as much needed coin and merchandise, stopping along the way there and back to trade at various ports in Africa or Asia where products such as sugar or tea could be got. When back in Australian waters she also worked the inter-colonial sea routes moving goods and people between Sydney and Hobart and other minor ports.

The 1827 destruction of the *Hope* was a significant shock to Hobart's population and to the colonial authorities who had been complacent regarding the safety of the entrance to Hobart's harbour, for the Derwent had developed an international reputation as one of the safest anchorages in the world. The wrecking of the *Hope* sullied this reputation and soon resulted in the erection of Hobart's first navigation light, which was built

---

[107] M. Bingham *Cascade, A taste of History* (Hobart) 1993 p.3
[108] H. O'May *Shipwrecks of Tasmania* (Hobart) 1954 p.14

on Iron Pot Island at the mouth of the Derwent River. It also resulted in the dismissal of the government pilot, Michael Mansfield, who, as a consequence, became the first European to settle and farm the Blackman's Bay area in Kingsborough, south of Hobart.[109] However these events occurred after Macintosh and Degraves had arrived in Hobart and are reasonably well documented. The purpose of this chapter is to examine the prior history of the *Hope* and explain how the present histories of this vessel came to contain errors that were the result of Degraves' deliberate actions. In particular this chapter will clarify issues related to the *Hope's* identity, age and ownership without which it is impossible to correctly navigate the conflicting accounts of her first abortive attempt to sail to Hobart in 1821 and the significant and far-reaching consequences of what followed.

The *Hope* was a sharply built, barque rigged, two decked, wooden sailing ship of 231 tons burthen built in Bristol in the year 1793 constructed of well seasoned English oak.[110] She was about the same size as Captain Cook's barque *Endeavour*, though of a very different shape.[111] The term "sharply built" implies a streamlined hull and a bow constructed for speed; the "sharply built" design was the precursor to the later clippers generally associated with design innovations that came out of North America (though this was not the case with the *Hope,* as she was specifically designated, by Lloyds' Insurance, as being built in Britain). A feature of the "sharp" design was that some storage space in the hull was sacrificed in the structural streamlining of the shape of the vessel, particularly at the bow; it was a feature that was to play an important part in the *Hope's* story.

---

[109] J. Gardam *A History of Brown's River* (Hobart) 1998 p.86
[110] *Lloyds'* Shipping Registers 1800-1819
[111] The word "burthen" is an old English word meaning "burden", referring to a ship's carrying capacity or tonnage. *Lloyds Register* 1800.

The fact that the *Hope* was built in Britain and of seasoned British oak was extremely important because these qualities were specifically required for her to obtain a "First Class" or "A1" rating with Lloyds' Insurance. This in turn determined the type of insured cargoes that the *Hope* could carry. First Class or A1 rated ships could be insured to carry any goods, including goods which might be "liable to sea (water) damage" (such as sugar). This was important because the *Hope* was originally and primarily employed in trading between the various British colonies in the Caribbean and ports in Britain and, occasionally, Canada, carrying a variety of cargoes, such as timber and tobacco. In her early years, however, her primary cargo was sugar—a product that spoiled easily if exposed to water.

Through the 17th and 18th centuries most of the European colonial powers attempted to acquire territories in the Caribbean in order to gain a stake in the lucrative sugar industry. The Netherlands, France, Spain and Britain all established plantation-based colonies there which relied almost exclusively on slave labour. After wresting Jamaica from the Spanish in the middle of the 17th century Britain set about to greatly increase her territorial holdings in the region through a series of treaties with France and the Netherlands which saw these nations ultimately cede to Britain the islands of St Lucia, Grenada, Dominica, St Vincent, Trinidad, Tobago and what was to become British Guiana. Through this period Britain also gained control over most of the Caribbean slave trade. These two combined factors gave her effective control of a large proportion of the world's sugar production.

For most of the 18th century British plantation owners and merchants made vast fortunes from the slave based sugar production using slave labour taken mostly from the West African coast. Whilst slave ships were specially built for carrying human cargo from the West Coast of Africa to the Caribbean's main slave markets in Jamaica, and did not engage in other trade, ships of the *Hope's* size and design, primarily used to carry general merchandise, often engaged in inter-colonial slave trading, carrying slaves from the main slave markets in Jamaica to sell in other ports around the Caribbean and the Americas as they picked up and discharged other cargoes.

The returns on investments (and in trade generally) in the West Indies remained high until the end of the 18th century when increased sugar production in other parts of the world, such as the Dutch East Indies, began to reduce prices in Europe. By the beginning of the 19th century the global depression of sugar prices combined with the 1807 abolition of the British slave trade to affect a severe down turn in the economies of the Caribbean colonies from which they would not recover for nearly two hundred years. The *Hope* began her life in the Caribbean just prior to this downturn.

The *Hope's* A1 rating lasted for 12 years after which time Lloyds' policies allowed that ships still "in perfect repair" could apply for an E1 or 2nd Class rating. The *Hope* was rated 2nd Class after 1805 but by 1819 she had lost her 2nd class rating and was downgraded to 3rd class, which meant that she could not be insured to carry goods that might be damaged by seawater. In other words she was leaking a lot.

Because she spent most of her life in tropical waters, the timber of the *Hope's* hull was under constant attack from the wood-eating, worm-like clam commonly known as the teredo worm or "shipworm". These tiny, invasive molluscs are often called the termites of the sea because the extensive damage that they cause often goes undetected: for, while the ship's hull may appear perfectly sound and undamaged, the internal timbers may be completely rotten, riddled with teredo worms. The reason for the undamaged appearance is that the teredo "worms" invade the timber of a ship when at an almost microscopic size during the free swimming stage of their life cycle. When they bore into the timber of the hull they leave only a tiny hole behind them. The presence of the worms is further concealed by the fact that their entrance hole is "hatched" by two "plates" which can be opened or closed by the worm. Once inside the hull the teredo worms bore into the timber allowing water into their burrow by controlling the "hatch" at the entrance through which a siphon extends, but which is withdrawn into the burrow if the worm is disturbed. The teredo worm, like the termite, eats the wood particles that its boring produces and also any microscopic creatures that enter its burrow. Though the entrance point may be microscopic the burrow itself is often over one centimetre in diameter. In cooler waters the burrows are rarely more than five or six centimetres in depth but in warmer tropical waters the teredo worm's burrow can often penetrate a ship's timber to a depth of two metres, causing severe structural damage. Teredos also grow very rapidly, whilst they are less than one quarter of a millimetre in length when they attach to a ship they can reach 10 centimetres in length after just one month inside a ship's hull.

Figure 34: The shipworm, correctly known as the Teredo Worm

Teredo worms were a serious problem for all ships that sailed tropical waters so the *Hope*, like Cook's *Endeavour* and other 18th century ships, was originally iron sheathed to provide a limited degree of protection against the worm's predations. Iron sheathing was a process whereby the section of the hull below the water line was coated with a mixture of tar and hair; this layer was then covered by planks of about half an inch thickness, then the planks were imbedded with thousands of broad headed nails so as to produce an "iron clad" effect. The nails were made of wrought iron which does not rust as rapidly as other forms of iron. This method was only effective until the salt water got past the layer of tar, which became brittle in colder waters and cracked under the stress of the normal flexing of the hull moving through waves. Once the tar cracked the intrusion of the salt water allowed access for the teredo worms which then bored into the wood of the hull and keel resulting in rot. This in turn caused more sections of tar to fall away allowing further entry of the wood boring worms into the ship's timbers. It was exactly this effect that forced Captain Cook to bring the *Endeavour* into Batavia for repairs and which ultimately resulted in the loss of a large number of the *Endeavour's* crew and company through disease.

The *Hope's* original iron sheathing was applied when she was built in 1793 and was replaced in 1801, then in 1812 the iron sheathing was removed and her hull was re-covered with copper sheathing. The copper sheathing of a ship involved the tacking of thin copper sheet to the exterior of a ship's hull. Although copper was very expensive in the 19th century, copper sheathing was so very much more effective than iron sheathing for preventing damage to the hull by worms and other agents that it easily justified the expense as the copper did not rust and only rarely cracked thus removing many of the problems associated with iron sheathing. As well as preventing the access of marine organisms to the hull's timber the copper sheathing had a chemical property that prevented marine plants from attaching to the hull. Because of these qualities the majority of shipping was copper sheathed by the middle of the 19th century.

Records of who originally built the *Hope* have not been found. The earliest records are in the Lloyds Insurance Registry of 1800; these show that in that year she was owned by of a person named Monckley and that her master was a Captain Wilson. It is likely that Monckley was the original owner and that he sold the *Hope* the year before she was to lose her A1 rating with Lloyds, in 1804. The *Hope's* ownership then passed to Gibbs & Company, the master being Captain Gardiner. Gibbs & Company owned her until 1814 when ownership passed to Hooper & Company who retained ownership until she was sold to Hugh Macintosh sometime in 1820. During the period between 1800 and 1820 the *Hope* appears to have sailed almost exclusively between Britain and various British ports around the Caribbean such as Barbados, Jamaica and Tobago.

In 1820 the *Hope* arrived in England on a run from Honduras carrying a primary cargo of mahogany timber for Hooper & Co under the command of Captain E. Seaton. Based on later testimonies, it is clear that Hooper & Co believed the *Hope's* days of sailing safely and profitably across the Atlantic were over; her copper sheathing was worn through in many places and due for replacement and the holes in the copper meant her hull would be riddled with teredo worm.[112] For these reasons Hooper & Co. sold their ship to Hugh Macintosh for just £850: the low price being indicative of the poor condition that the *Hope* was in at the time of purchase.

At that time, a reasonable price for a second-hand sailing ship of 231 tons burthen in good condition was between £2,500 and £3,000. A good example of this is again Cook's *Endeavour*, which was just over three years old when purchased by the Navy in 1768 for £2,800. Prices were normally worked out at a price per ton rate, with a price of around £10 per ton of capacity (burthen) for a new ship. Hence the *Endeavour,* being of 368 tons burthen and just over three years old, sold for just under eight pounds per ton. This price was for a relatively new ship in good condition, with the term "good condition" being primarily related to the condition of the hull. By comparison the *Hope* sold for under £3 per ton. As the price per ton did not usually include the rigging and such things as anchors, cable and other

---

[112] *London Times* 6th March 1823 p. 4

extras, only the cost of the actual ship, it is clear that the *Hope,* which came with rigging, was sold at a knock-down price.

By 1820 the *Hope* was 27 years old; an old, worm-riddled, ship with significant structural problems, including worn copper sheathing, a rotten keel and rotting timbers in her hull, the result of her years plying the tropical waters of the Caribbean, nineteen of those years being without the protection of copper sheathing. Lloyds' Register records show that from 1802 to 1821 she had required notable repair work every year and, whilst the records do not show the exact details of these repairs, annotations show that this work was often of a major nature.

Generally the existing literature on the *Hope* and Peter Degraves states either that Degraves and Macintosh, or Degraves on his own purchased the *Hope* for the specific purpose of transporting themselves and their families, plus a load of paying passengers and a substantial quantity of machinery, equipment and merchandise to Hobart Town in Van Dieman's Land. Other writers claim either that Degraves chartered the *Hope*, or was allowed to use it by the trustee of his creditors. Contemporaries were also under the impression that the ship was jointly owned. Mary Reibey (the ex-convict who became one of Sydney's first successful business women) was in London in the early 1820s.[113] She had returned to the "old country" on an extended tour with her daughters during which she had also purchased goods not easily obtainable in Sydney. In early 1821 she had returned to London from Glasgow and was residing near the London docks. Through February and March she spent some of her time inspecting ships to select a suitable vessel for her return

---

[113] Mary Reibey was born in 1777 in Lancashire, England. At age 13, an orphan living with her grandmother, she was convicted of horse stealing and sentenced to be transported for seven years. She arrived in Sydney in 1792. In September 1794 she married Thomas Reibey, a young Irishman who had worked for the East India Company. They began a number of business and trading ventures together. When Thomas died Mary took over the businesses, which continued to thrive.

voyage. She inspected the *Hope* and on several occasions and dined with Macintosh and Degraves. In her journal Mrs Reibey leaves no doubt that, in her mind, Macintosh and Degraves were joint owners of the *Hope*. Yet despite Reibey's impression the records from Lloyds' Insurance Register for the period show unambiguously that Macintosh was the sole owner of the *Hope* from 1821 to 1826.[114] If in 1821 most people who had dealings with Degraves or the *Hope* were under the impression that Degraves was the owner, or at least the principle owner, the modern confusion about the ownership of the *Hope* is understandable.[115] Yet while giving people the impression he owned the *Hope*, Degraves also made a deliberate effort to obscure and confuse her identity and origins by altering details in the documents associated with her re-insurance with Lloyds. He did so to avoid having her seized by creditors.

Regardless of who actually owned the *Hope* Degraves was certainly the principle instigator in the events that followed her purchase. There can also be no doubt that he was short of cash and that he sought further finance for his project by maximising the number of fare paying passengers that could be put on board the ship. To this end a ship joiner, John Forsyth, was employed to build extra cabins between the *Hope's* two decks, substantially reducing storage space below decks but significantly increasing the potential for immediate income from passengers who had to pay cash up front to book their passage. The alterations to the *Hope* were carried out in London in the Lime-house Canal which still joins the Thames near the docks at Blackwall.[116] While the work being done in the canal increased the *Hope's* passenger carrying capacity, Degraves refused to

---

[114] There were various reasons for the apparent inconsistencies, which are related to the numerous court actions that Peter Degraves was involved in at that period of time, but these issues are complex and will be dealt with specifically in the following chapter.
[115] P. Walker *All We Inherit* (Hobart) 1968
[116] M. Reibey *Journal 1820-21* 16th February 1821

spend money on the much needed structural repairs that the aging vessel required before attempting the long and dangerous voyage to Van Diemen's Land.

Figure 35: Limehouse Canal in London runs directly off the Thames River and was where the *Hope* was taken to be refitted in 1820 and also where Hugh Macintosh and Mary Reibey met, on board the *Hope*.

So it was that by the middle of 1821 the *Hope* was transformed from being a ship principally designed for carrying cargo to a ship that could carry some cargo and a very large number of paying passengers. At the same time it was Degraves' unwillingness to make those structural repairs to the ship worm infested hull that almost fatally interrupted the *Hope's* first voyage to Van Diemen's Land and led to her being seized by the British port authorities.

Chapter Eleven: Refitting and Finances

> Called on Captain Macintosh who lives in Ratcliffe Highway, he having purchased a ship called the *Hope*, and intending to take passengers to N. S. Wales. He called a Coach and we went on board; she is lying in the Canal refitting but she appeared to be longer before she will sail than I wish to stop I can make no agreement. The other half owner, Degraves, being on board he also is going out with his family to settle at V. Diemen's Land. (They) wished for all the information I could give them which I did to best of my judgment. Captain Macintosh appears to be quite the Gentleman. We all walked back calling in our way at a pastry cook's shop and taking refreshment we parted and each party went their own way after they giving me an invitation to Dine with them. Went home and Dined after took a walk in the Minories and made some purchases.

Mary Reibey's Journal: Friday 16th February 1821

The close of 1820 saw Peter Degraves and Hugh Macintosh living in London near to where the *Hope* was standing at dock, in Limehouse Canal, being refurbished. Macintosh had taken lodgings on the Ratcliffe Highway so he could be close to where the *Hope* was docked. The Ratcliffe Highway (now known as St George's Street) ran alongside of the London dockside area of Wapping and was a place of lodgings and other establishments that serviced the needs of sailors and visitors to the docks. Degraves lodged his family across the Thames in Neptune Street, Southwark, also only a short distance from where the *Hope* was berthed. Peter and Sophia Degraves now had seven children. Interestingly, not long after arriving back in London, he and Sophia had all their children "re-baptised" *en masse* at the Anglican Church of St George the Martyr in Holborn. This was the same church in which Degraves' brother Henry had been baptised and where Degraves' elder children had also been baptised before he fled to Scotland. There is no clear reason for this "re-baptism" though, with the family's awareness of the dangers of their upcoming journey to Hobart, it is reminiscent of the baptism of Macintosh's son William immediately prior to his return to England. Parents wanted to be certain that if their children died on the long ocean voyage, and there was a good chance they would, that they would be sure to gain entrance to Heaven.

It is largely from the 1820-1821 journal of Mary Reibey, the ex-convict whose face now adorns the Australian $20 note, that we gain an insight into what Macintosh and Degraves were doing in early 1821. Mary Reibey was one year younger than Macintosh and had been sentenced to be transported to Sydney, aged 13, for supposedly stealing a horse. It was a severe sentence and it has been argued that female felons, such as Reibey, frequently received the sentence of transportation to Australia for minor offences to help balance the chronic shortage of women there. Four years later, she married Thomas Reibey, a young Scottish civilian officer of the East India Company, whom she met on the ship that had transported her to Australia. Together the pair ran a number of successful business enterprises in Sydney of which, after her husband's early death, Mary became the sole proprietor. In late 1819, as a rich widow in her early 40s, she took her daughters back to England and Scotland to visit their family. They arrived in Portsmouth in June 1820.

After a period in Glasgow visiting and acquainting her daughters with their departed father's family Reibey returned to London in 1821 and, like Macintosh, took lodgings near the London docks in order to seek a suitable ship to take her back to Sydney. It was there that she made her acquaintance with Macintosh and was obviously taken by him for they began to meet frequently. Over the weeks which followed the acquaintance between Macintosh and Reibey became quite intimate and, ultimately, it was to stretch over a number of years. Reibey may have been of working class origins, but she was now a wealthy, good looking widow, in her early forties, who was returning to the colonies where she was an important member of society. Macintosh, on the other hand, was a distinguished widower, an officer and a gentleman, with upper class origins who happened to be of similar age and was bound for the same colonial outpost to start a new life.

Figure 36: This image of Mary Reibey is taken from the only known painting of her, a miniature made when she was 58, 15 years after she met Macintosh in London. Her image now adorns Australia's $20 notes.

Exactly when Mary Reibey and Hugh Macintosh first met we do not know. Reibey first mentions him in her journal entry for the Friday 16th February 1821 when she visited him at his Ratcliffe Highway lodgings from whence they took a coach down to inspect the *Hope* at Limehouse Canal. Mrs Reibey, whose businesses included shipping, immediately saw that the refurbishments to the *Hope* would have the ship in dock much longer than she was prepared to wait in London. Though she had no further interest in the *Hope* Reibey's interest in Macintosh grew. Leaving the *Hope* they went for a walk together ending up at a pastry shop where they "took refreshments" and then parted, though only after making a date to meet again for dinner.

Over the following weeks, Macintosh and Mary Reibey met a number of times, dining or taking tea together. On Sunday, 25 February, they dined with Peter and Sophia Degraves. After their meal Mary stayed on into the evening and was then walked back to her lodgings by Macintosh. Two weeks later, hearing that Macintosh was very ill, she called on him again at his lodgings where she found him being nursed by his sister Sophia. The visit was repeated two days later and she again spent time with him and his sister. There can be no doubt Macintosh would have impressed Mary with his refined manners and tales of the exotic worlds of India and Persia. At the same time she would have told him of life in the colonies and the great opportunities to be found there.

Figure 37: Early photograph of Ratcliffe Highway where Macintosh lived while the _Hope_ was being refitted. This area provided for the needs of ships and also of sailors, including bars, brothels and opium dens.

Reibey and Macintosh continued to develop their relationship for four months until, after almost exactly one year in Britain, Mary sailed for Sydney on board the *Mariner*. Her last meeting with Macintosh was on the 7th June 1821 on board the *Hope* on the day of her departure. At that last meeting there can be no doubt Macintosh promised he would visit Mary at her home in Sydney as soon as the *Hope* reached the Australia, for the expectation of Macintosh, at this time, was that he would be sailing to Australia within a few months. And Macintosh did visit Mary Reibey in Sydney when he eventually arrived in the Antipodes, though the delay was to be years, not the months that the two lovers had expected.

At the time Mary Reibey bid farewell to Macintosh on the decks of the *Hope*, in June 1821, Macintosh and Degraves appeared to be well on the way to achieving their goals. Work on the *Hope* was nearing completion and her hold was being filled with the machinery and agricultural equipment each man would need to fulfil their dreams.[117]

Degraves' plan was to first build a sawmill, then a flour mill, and then make the most of whatever other opportunities to make money presented themselves. However there were two significant obstacles for Degraves, one was the lack of capital, a problem that he had only partially solved by bringing in his brother-in-law as a partner. The other was his past, which he went to great lengths to obscure, particuarly his bankrupcy. With his supposed part ownership of the *Hope* as evidence of capital and with his convincing ability to bend the truth, Degraves was able to obtain credit from tradesmen and merchants for much of the machinery and other equipment he needed which Macintosh could not or would not pay for.

---

[117] Hugh Macintosh to Bathurst 20th June 1821: C.O. 201/106 'M'

Macintosh's dreams of a new life in Van Diemen's Land were very different from those of his brother-in-law. He was an capitalist not an industrialist, he expected his captital to do the work and for his investment in Degraves' project to provide him with an income. Like many of the "genteel poor" Macintosh wanted land and a lifestyle that he could not hope for in Britain. He saw his involvement as Degraves' partner in the milling projects as an investment that would give him a return on his capital while he pursued his agricultural interests. To this end he had spent those funds that remained after the purchase and refitting of the *Hope* on items related to agriculture. The basis of Macintosh's new life in Van Deiman's Land was to be his "...fine merino sheep and Yorkshire cattle and a selection of French vines." All of which he had purchased and ready to bring on board the *Hope.*

Through most of the 1820s the British government actively encouraged men with capital to migrate to Australia. One of the incentives to encourage such persons was the possibility of a land grant of up to 2000 acres. Degraves and Macintosh made separate applications which were representative of the difference in their long term plans for their new life. Degraves wanted land with stands of the tall timber that he had heard covered the slopes of Mount Wellington to the south of Hobart. Macintosh's requirements were very different; he wanted rich agricultural land where he could, with the help of the "seven servants of various occupations" he was bringing with him as well as convict labour, establish an agricultural estate. It was Macintosh's dream to establish Hobart's first vineyards.

At this point it is also worth considering the issue of who was the senior partner in what was to become the Cascade Empire, for the significance of Macintosh's position and his contribution is a contentious one as there is an almost universal assumption that Degraves was the senior partner. Existing histories such as those by Allport, Bingham and Hooper largely ignore

Macintosh's contributions, as does the existing promotional material placed in the public domain today by the Cascade Brewery and associated organisations. There are several pieces of evidence that prove Macintosh's position in the partnership was that of senior partner. Perhaps the strongest comes from the Macintosh and Degraves silver shilling, which was minted in the Boulton Mint at Soho.

Although the coin was stamped with the date 1823, Macintosh and Degraves probably hit upon the scheme of making the tokens after talking with Mary Reibey in 1821 who would have alerted them to the chronic shortage of hard cash in Sydney and Hobart. The coin itself is of great interest historically because it is generally acknowledged to be the first piece of decorative art to use the word Tasmania to describe Van Diemen's Land and also the first piece of decorative art to use the image of a kangaroo.

Figure 38: The now rare Macintosh and Degraves silver shilling. When the 3,000 coins were minted Tasmania was still known as Van Diemen's Land and was not officially named Tasmania until 1856. In 2012 one of these coins sold for $26,000, only a handful are known to still exist, the fate of the bulk of the coins is not known.

The coin is now generally called the "Degraves Shilling" and it is generally held that Degraves had it made. This convention of naming the coin thus is an example of how thoroughly Degraves placed his stamp upon history, even though the inscription on the coin says "Macintosh and Degraves Saw Mills" and the placement of Macintosh's name first is a clear indication of prominence in the partnership, which is supported by the fact that he was the sole registered owner of the *Hope*. And although many modern authorities ascribe the manufacture of this coin to Degraves, it is more likely that Macintosh was responsible, especially since they were made at the Soho Mint, which was owned by Matthew Boulton who was a close friend and associate of Macintosh's father-in-law, William Nicholson. There were reportedly 2,000 of these silver shillings minted, which would have probably cost Macintosh around £150. Further evidence for Macintosh's prominence in the partnership is the fact that all correspondence to the Colonial Office and other government authorities that concerned their joint enterprise was always signed "Macintosh and Degraves", always with Macintosh's name placed first, even when Degraves was the author.

By the time that the *Hope* had been refitted and ready to sail, both men had invested a large portion of their available funds into the venture. How much they actually spent is not clear, particularly in Degraves' case where the evidence suggests that his actual cash investment was probably very little. In the case of Macintosh, various documents mention the amount of capital that he invested in the expedition was upwards of five or six thousand pounds, which included livestock and equipment to start life as a pastoralist in Australia.[118] They later claimed to

---

[118] D.S. MacMillan states Macintosh had capital £5,000 plus half ownership of the *Hope*. The *Times* in 1823 records a total investment by Macintosh of around £6,000 plus the *Hope*, while Degraves, in his petition to the Lords of Admiralty mentions a figure of £7,000 including the *Hope*.

have spent £3,000 refitting the *Hope*, though this amount would seem to be excessive given later testimony and that the original cost of the vessel was only £850. It is more likely that the total cost of the *Hope*, including the refitting, would have been somewhat less than £2,000. Apart from his supposed half share in the *Hope*, Degraves claimed to have invested around £3,000 in machinery to take to Hobart, although this amount is also likely to be inflated as a result of three separate compensation claims that will be described later.[119] Macintosh himself in a letter to Lord Bathurst dated 20th June 1821, says that even after purchasing the *Hope*, his animals, plants and agricultural machinery, he still had "disposable capital of rather more than £5,000".

Apart from being certain that Macintosh had plenty of capital and Degraves did not the exact state of the two men's finances is very difficult to establish. Degraves would certainly have hidden his debts and lack of capital as the amount of capital determined the size of the land grant a new settler could expect. For this reason it was a common ploy of colonists to inflate the size of their capital assets as a means to maximise the amount of land they would be granted.

Whilst Macintosh supplied most of the cash for the project Degraves appears to have made his contributions "in kind" with equipment (mostly purchased on credit) and the promise that his expertise would have a tangible value once they arrived in Hobart. It is also likely that Macintosh was not actually aware of the extent of Degraves' debts or his chronic shortage of cash. And of course Degraves had never been one to let lack of money be an obstacle to his plans so, like his father, he obtained as much credit as he could for his machinery and other purchases and then improved his cash reserves by getting as many fare-paying passengers on board the *Hope* as was possible. By

---

[119] *London Times* 6th March 1823 p.4

altering the ship so it could carry about 90 passengers, with fares of between £30 to £50 per adult, the partners would have expected to make somewhere around £2,500 profit after the cost of buying provisions. [120] The job of selling fares and other arrangements to do with the needs of the passengers naturally fell to Degraves who, like his father, was a clever and convincing communicator and well capable of learning and practicing those tactics and deceptions already in use to exploit potential immigrants. For Degraves the critical factor was to leave London with the maximum number of paying passengers who would then be fed at the lowest cost.

---

[120] *London Courier* 3rd January 1822; *London Times* 6th March 1823 p.4

Chapter Twelve: The Hopeful Emigrants

Around April or May 1821 Peter Degraves heard of a large group of Wesleyans who were planning to migrate to Van Diemen's Land and were looking for a suitable ship to take them. These Wesleyans were intent on sailing to Hobart to join a congregation of family and friends who had already established themselves there.[121]

The Wesleyan movement was originally made up of members of the Church of England who sought a more personalised religious experience than was generally offered within the ritualised services of their Church. Founded by the brothers John and Charles Wesley in the middle of the 18th century as the result of a shared religious experience, which occurred while they were both clergymen of the Church of England, the movement had the evangelical focus of spreading scriptural holiness across Britain. Whilst there had been no original intention of founding a separate denomination, John Wesley's strong emphasis on his followers having a personal religious experience and on striving for "Christian perfection" (a phrase which was intended to imply that all thoughts, words and actions should be governed by adherence to the scriptures and by "holy love") ensured such an outcome by the 1790's. By 1820 the number of Wesleyans in Britain numbered over 200,000 and, with the movement's emphasis on evangelical and missionary activities, considerable numbers of Wesleyans had migrated to British colonies around the world. Whilst the overt "collective" motive behind the Wesleyans' intention to move to Van Diemen's Land was of an essentially missionary or evangelical nature and influenced by

---

[121] Whilst in the latter part of the 18th century and early 19th century members of this religious movement were generally known as Wesleyans, after the two brothers Wesley who were the founders, they later adopted the name Methodists, by which name they were known through the 20th century until combining with other Protestant congregations to form the Uniting Church.

the letters of Reverend William Horton, the Wesleyan missionary in Hobart, most also had personal reasons for making such a momentous move.

When Degraves heard about the intended mass migration, he immediately set about convincing this little congregation to book their passage on the *Hope* with what was from, all existing accounts, a sustained sales campaign aimed at the most influential members of the group. Degraves regularly visited the Wesleyan leaders at their homes to push the benefits of booking passage for the whole group on his ship and he represented the conditions on board the *Hope* "in glowing terms".

Figure 39: John Wesley, founder of the Methodists, was first a minister in the Church of England. His followers were known as Wesleyans.

It was a ship, he claimed, with the space, facilities and provisions to enable the Wesleyan families to make the long, arduous journey to Hobart in relative safety and comfort. In particular Degraves focused his attentions on one man in the "influential" group, Robert Mather, a successful Scot from Lauder whose father had been a blacksmith. Mather moved to London in about 1795 to take up an apprenticeship with to a hosier named Romanes, also a Scot. Not long after Mather completed his seven year apprenticeship his master decided to go into semi-retirement and left Robert Mather in charge of his business. Eventually Mather took over the business, in which he prospered and grew to a point where he took up a larger shop at 20 Sun Street' Bishopsgate in London. Apart from being a successful shop keeper he was the superintendent of a Wesleyan Sunday School in London and the son-in-law of the highly respected Wesleyan missionary and editor of the Wesleyan's national magazine, Reverend J. Benson. Mather met Benson's daughter, Anne, at the Wesleyan Sunday school where they both taught. There appears to have been some initial resistance from the Benson family, who owned houses and property in Leeds, to the prospect of their daughter marrying a shopkeeper, but the devout nature of their prospective son-in-law appears to have overcome their social prejudices.

Mather's reason for deciding to sell his successful business and take his family out of London was primarily due to the illness of his wife; however behind this was a desire common to many free settlers in the colonies, the possibility of becoming a landowner and thereby transcending his working class origins. His views and expectations of life in Van Diemen's Land were influenced by the books of William Wentworth: *A Statistical Account of the British Settlements in Australasia* (1819) and Captain Jeffreys': *Geographical and Descriptive Delineations of the Island of Van Diemen's Land* (1820), which had just been published. Mather was also influenced by face to face discussions he had with Wentworth himself. These accounts of the colonial life gave very positive, if not entirely accurate, impressions of the climate, resources and opportunities that existed for enterprising people with the capital to progress their fortunes.[122] Both the books spoke highly of the advantageous climate in the colonies, particularly in Van Diemen's Land. The supposedly healthy nature of the Van Diemen's Land's climate was an important factor in Robert Mather's deliberations, for Anne's health deteriorated after the birth of their first child, Sarah, and Robert became convinced that his wife's constitution was not robust enough to cope with the polluted city air which was becoming an increasing problem for its residents as the city became more and more industrialised. On the advice of their family doctor Mrs Mather took regular extended trips to stay by the English seaside where her health improved immediately only to deteriorate upon returning to the family home in London. Mather had originally intended to solve this problem by buying a business in one of the sea side towns such as Portsmouth or Ramsgate and moving himself and his family there, but after extensive searching he could find nothing suitable. He was already aware that other Wesleyans, including some close personal friends, had moved to Van Diemen's Land and were doing quite well there in various fields of endeavour. So when he heard members of his congregation were planning to move to the distant colony he joined with them to investigate the options available for transplanting his own family.

As the idea of a mass relocation grew amongst his friends Mather brought together a group of successful Wesleyan luminaries to form a committee to ensure the correct choice of a vessel for the passage. Degraves' regular visits to Mather's family home, where he spruiked the benefits of taking passage on the *Hope,* are recorded in the memoirs of his daughter Sarah Benson-Walker (nee Mather), mother of the 19th century Tasmanian historian Peter Backhouse Walker. Through persistence and extravagant promises he had no intention of keeping, Degraves eventually convinced Mather and the other

---

[122] Macintosh and Degraves would also have read these same books.

committee members to book and pay for their group's passage to Hobart on the *Hope*. Whilst most of the congregation would travel steerage, Robert Mather engaged with Degraves to travel in the relative comfort of "cabin class" (the early 19th century equivalent of today's first class) for the benefit of his ill wife, as he was able to afford the considerably higher fares. Like his fellows he paid a significant deposit in advance to secure his passage booking himself and his family into the *Hope's* largest cabin.

The Wesleyan emigrants with whom Mather had joined were a mix of people from various professions and social classes who travelled mainly as steerage passengers. Despite the difference in social class and wealth the group was closely bonded by their shared belief in Christian fellowship and the importance of living scrupulously honest and spiritual lives. The committee which represented them consisted of six men. While it had originally been formed to make the choice of which ship the group should embark on it also oversaw the various necessary negotiations with Degraves prior to making a down payment on their fares. As well as Mather, the committee included Mr John Dean, Mr Whyhall, Mr Jones, William Shoobridge and Joshua Drabble. [123] After several meetings through May and June in 1821 (some of the minutes of which still survive) the committee came to an agreement with Degraves that the Wesleyans would pay ten percent of their fares in advance, at the time of booking their passage, and pay the balance immediately prior to boarding. However, whilst Degraves initially agreed to those terms, it appears that they did not remain acceptable to him for long. Somehow he contrived to renegotiate their agreement and

---

[123] Shoobridge, after his arrival in Hobart, was initially persuaded by Governor Sorrel to become the superintendent of the government timber yards in Hobart. However he quit after a few years and devoted himself to growing hops. Drabble became the superintendent of the infamous Hobart Female Factory.

managed to get between 50% and 100% of their fares in advance payments—testimony both to Degraves' persuasive powers and of his urgent need for ready cash.

Around the time these negotiations were taking place Degraves and Macintosh engaged Captain Francis Allison as the *Hope*'s master for the voyage. Various contemporary accounts seem to suggest that Degraves may have negotiated some kind of deal in lieu of wages with Captain Allison, as the passengers' letters and notes indicate that Allison had shipped 50 tons of his own trade merchandise as freight aboard the *Hope,* that 50 tons representing about one quarter of the *Hope's* total capacity .

After protracted negotiations and having received numerous verbal and written assurances from Degraves, the passengers arrived at the London docks early in August 1821 ready to move their goods and chattels on board in preparation for their departure before the end of August, the date agreed to by Degraves. This sailing date was important in order to avoid the storm season which traditionally began around the equinox which in 1821 would fall on the 14th of September. When the passengers arrived at the docks, they were told that there were unexpected delays and that they could not board the ship for at least several weeks. Worse news was to follow, because of shortage of space they were also told that much of their freight could not be placed on the *Hope.*

The issue of freight was of great importance to all free settlers with capital as, prior to departing England, they generally converted their cash into trade goods that were known to be in demand in the colonies. These goods, such as shoes or cloth or tools, could then be sold for considerable profit on arrival and the new settlers could thereby increase the capital available for whatever long-term venture they had planned.

The unexpected delay and the lack of storage space necessitated some quick work by the Wesleyans to find another ship able to take the balance of their freight so that it would arrive in Hobart at approximately the same time as the *Hope*. To arrive in Van Diemen's Land with only a portion of one's possessions and have to wait around for their arrival was undesirable, yet the alternative of having them arrive some time prior to the disembarkation of their owners was even less desirable as it would invite pilfering. The delay presented a particular and major problem for William Shoobridge whose freight included a significant number of hops plants and cuttings with which he hoped to establish agricultural production to supply the colony's beer brewers. The hops would not survive a long delay in London. Degraves made it clear that there was no choice in the matter so the committee did the best it could on short notice and organised for a considerable quantity of the Wesleyans' freight to be sent on to Hobart on another ship, the *Denmark Hill*. Unfortunately the latter was not scheduled to leave London until around the end of 1821 and so would arrive in Hobart several months after the *Hope*, leaving the emigrants without many of the items they would need to establish their new lives, though ultimately this turned out to be the least of their problems.

It was mid-October before the passengers were eventually able to board the *Hope*, almost two months after the promised departure date and well into the storm season. Once on board it quickly became obvious that conditions were not as Degraves had promised they would be. He had, at their various meetings assured the wary and economically conservative Wesleyans that the *Hope* was a top-class vessel that was well-suited for the long voyage and possessed of adequate space to ensure the comfort of even the steerage passengers and their children. The God-fearing Wesleyans had taken Degraves on his word, both spoken and written, and had expected him, as a gentleman, to honour his promises.[124] However as the Wesleyans boarded the *Hope* they saw decks crowded with crates and other freight, including Macintosh's Merino sheep, his Yorkshire cattle and probably a horse or two. When the steerage passengers climbed down the ladder to enter their quarters below deck, they discovered that conditions in that dark space were cramped beyond any reasonable expectation. Even the cabin passengers, who had paid premium prices for their passage, made similarly distressing discoveries of Degraves' deceptions as they were directed to cabins that bore little resemblance to those that had been promised. For example, Robert Mather had been relegated to a much smaller cabin than the one he had previously been shown by Degraves and for which he had paid the full fare of £263.10.6, in advance, in order to secure the most comfortable passage for his ailing wife and young children. To make matters worse, Mather soon discovered that the cabin he had been promised was occupied by Degraves and his family and that they had no intention of moving out.

Accommodation for the steerage passengers was much worse. Indeed the space was so cramped that they did not even have enough room to set up a table to eat off. A number were forced to sleep on the floor; there not being sufficient space to hang a hammock. Conditions became even worse when on the night before the ship was due to leave London the sleeping passengers were disturbed by dock workers moving more crates of goods and equipment (belonging to Degraves, Macintosh and Captain Allison) on board the already overcrowded ship.

The next morning, the passengers' committee met to organise a letter of complaint to the Lord Mayor of London about conditions aboard the ship, but before this could be delivered Captain Allison took the *Hope* down the Thames and into the

---

[124] Minutes of Committee Meeting June 29th 1821 Utas Archives M10/1

English Channel headed for Lands End and the vast expanses of the Atlantic Ocean where the Captain's word was the law.

With no other options open to them, they made a formal, but impotent complaint to Degraves who dismissed them out of hand. Next they tried Captain Allison who said he was bound to act on the owners' orders. Finally they went to Macintosh whom they considered to be an honourable man and who, like them, had also been duped by the unscrupulous Degraves.[125] It appears that Macintosh attempted to act as a mediator however Degraves refused to speak to any deputation from the passengers; nor would he make any concessions to any of the demands put to him. This placed Macintosh in a difficult position. He had invested heavily in the ship and the expedition on the basis of Degraves' enthusiasm and optimistic arguments. It is indeed likely that up until the voyage had actually begun, Macintosh had little understanding of the scale of the deception that his brother-in-law wrought upon the unfortunate Wesleyans. But now confined in the small ship that carried his fortune and future he found himself surrounded with the irrefutable evidence that his partner and brother-in-law was a rouge and a scoundrel. Macintosh must have known that, once again, there was nothing he could do but play the hand that fate had dealt him. No doubt he recalled the day when, outside the gates of Seringapatam, he had been forced to turn and fight against the British troops sent to stop him, knowing that, not only was this a battle that he could not win, but that his fellow mutineers within the walls of Seringapatam were not going to leave the safety of the fortress to rescue him. As the *Hope* sailed into the English Channel Macintosh knew he could neither help the passengers or himself if he began a battle with Degraves so from then until they arrived in Hobart three years later he abided by his brother-in-law's tactics—he had little option to do otherwise.

---

[125] R. Mather *A few of the particulars of what has passed between the Captain and owners of the Hope.*

Without Macintosh's support it became clear to the passengers that there was nothing they could do other than to make the best of a bad situation and endure the cramped conditions on the ship with fortitude knowing that the voyage to Hobart would be a long and uncomfortable one. Only a few days later, however, they discovered further deceptions which made their already difficult circumstances far more precarious.

In the course of the negotiations with Degraves the Wesleyans had agreed on a set of basic requirements that would be guaranteed before they would pay him the portion of their fare money which he required as a deposit. These included that the *Hope* be surveyed by an independent shipping surveyor, chosen by the Wesleyans, but at Degraves' expense. Somehow, however, Degraves managed to avoid this. Another requirement was that the ship should "leave the Lizard by the 1st of September" to avoid the storm season; again Degraves failed to keep his promise. Lastly they required a written list of the provisions, including food, water, wine and spirits, which would be available to both steerage and cabin passengers on a daily basis throughout the voyage. Degraves supplied such a list, which guaranteed generous portions of good-quality provisions, the cost of which was included in the fare. No doubt having calculated that they would be well away from English shores before the passengers discovered the true and meagre extent of the ship's victualling, Degraves reneged on this too. Luckily for the passengers, however, nature intervened.[126]

---

[126] In fact supplying seriously sub-standard provisions was a regular deception practiced on migrant passengers by unscrupulous ship owners. By interesting coincidence Mary Reibey suffered from the same scam on her journey back to Sydney in the *Mariner*. In Reibey's case the deception was discovered a couple of weeks into the trip. The *Mariner* was forced to sail into port where the passengers pooled their money and reprovisioned the ship themselves.

After only two days at sea their ship was caught in a terrible and prolonged storm that caused considerable damage to the *Hope* as well as to other shipping in the Channel. Captain Allison sought shelter from the gale force winds and crashing waves by anchoring behind the Goodwin Sands off the Downs. This was normal practice although the Sands were, and still are, a well known graveyard for shipping. Although partially sheltered from the storm it was not long before the *Hope* began leaking at an alarming rate and the passengers became aware of the ship's severe structural problems.

Figure 40: The Goodwin Sands, in the English Channel east of Ramsgate, was both a place where ships sheltered from storms and a place where they were wrecked by storms. Ships are still wrecked there today.

Anchored at sea in a leaking ship, locked below decks, pounded by wild winds and high seas, the dismayed Wesleyans discovered the next of Degraves' deceptions—the promised rations failed to materialise. In steerage, after only a week at sea, the children were crying from hunger. It transpired that their total daily food intake consisted of "only one small cup of tea and a piece of brown biscuit for breakfast and supper and about half a pint of brown barley and carrot broth with a grain of oatmeal in it." The wealthier passengers who dined in the cabin fared little better, for both the quality and quantity of the food provided was so far below the standard promised that Captain Allison was too embarrassed to sit down at the same table with them. However, as events transpired, it was fortunate for the Wesleyan emigrants that the *Hope* had been caught in the storm whilst still in English waters, for the damage, including the loss of both her anchors and the destruction of the windlass, was so substantial that it forced Allison to run for repairs and shelter in Royal Ramsgate Harbour.

Figure 41: Sarah Benson-Walker was Robert Mather's eldest daughter. Sarah was about 10 years old when she and her family boarded the ill fated voyage of the *Hope*. Her recollections of the voyage make fascinating reading.

Once in harbour the distressed passengers, who had by now run out of such basic requirements as candles and coal for their cooking stoves, complained to the Ramsgate authorities that the ship was unseaworthy, overloaded with both cargo and passengers and under-provisioned. Customs Officers who inspected the ship upheld their claims and the *Hope* was impounded whilst Degraves and Macintosh were arrested for breach of the Passengers Act. Mr K.B. Martin, deputy harbour master of Ramsgate, took control of the *Hope* and placed her in a docking area for damaged ships. This duty required the *Hope* to be "lay …on the ground" where she would not sink. The *Hope* was taken into the docks on the high tide to a preselected location where she was settled onto a bed of mud about one and a half feet deep, with the passengers and their goods still on board.

Once the *Hope* had been seized protracted legal manoeuvrings began between her owners and the passengers during which all parties obtained legal advice and used whatever influence they could muster to achieve their desired goals. For the passengers, the initial goal was to get the *Hope* to a seaworthy state and so resume their voyage, their committee even going so far as to offer to lend money to Macintosh (whom they still believed to be an honourable man) to have the ship repaired and got under way. However, it soon became clear that this was not likely to happen given the extent of the repairs required and the confrontational attitude adopted by Degraves, who was seeking legal advice on how to have the passengers forcibly removed from his ship. After being made aware of Degraves' plans, the Wesleyans switched their efforts to trying to retrieve their passage money, the five pounds per ton paid for freight and their actual goods that were stowed below the *Hope's* decks. With limited options and holding to the old adage that "possession is nine tenths of the Law" the passengers refused to leave the ship until their money and goods were returned to them. Without their passage money and their goods most would have been rendered destitute and unable to either continue on their journey or to re-establish themselves in England.

The priorities of Macintosh and Degraves were very different. The first was to get themselves out of jail and their ship released by customs; next was to retain the passengers' money; and then to get the *Hope* repaired through their insurance policy with Lloyds. Once these goals were achieved their plan was to get the *Hope* out of Ramsgate and be under way as quickly as possible for Hobart. There were several reasons for this, not least of which was the fact that the creditors who had been pursuing Degraves for payment of outstanding bills had learned he was intent on leaving the country.

Some time during these complex manoeuvrings Captain Allison, appalled by Degraves' behaviour, resigned his position—an action that the now slightly paranoid Degraves believed proved that Allison was in league with, or even the leader of, the passengers' revolt.[127] Allison was replaced, on paper at least, by a Captain J.H. Duke, a man unknown to the passengers and who appears to never have actually trod the decks of the *Hope*. It appears from Degraves' later letters, written from jail in Hobart Town, that Captain Duke was both Degraves' London agent and a friend or long-standing business associate upon whom Degraves could rely to do whatever he required in the way of putting false information on government paperwork.

The *Hope* and her passengers remained in Ramsgate as weeks dragged into months. And while Degraves continued to refuse to return their fare and freight money he continued to plan a way to get the passengers off his ship. But the Wesleyans stayed put and would not be moved, for they had no other option. Without the return of their money they would be stuck in England with the merchandise they had intended to sell for profit in the colonies. That same merchandise, if sold in England, could only be sold for a loss. On top of this, they had all quit their jobs, sold

---

[127] *Memorial to the Directors of the Honourable East India Company from Hugh Macintosh*

their businesses, vacated their homes and invested their life's savings in the move to Van Diemen's Land. To remain in England would have ruined them, so they had little choice but to stay on board the *Hope* and work for some form of resolution.

Trapped on board the ship, the passengers began an extensive cycle of prayer by hoisting the Bethel Flag up the *Hope's* mast. In the 19th century this flag was used to indicate that a church service was taking place on board a ship and with the Bethel Flag they invited other religious persons passing by to join them in prayer for a speedy resolution of their plight. And come they did. The Wesleyans' plight became a *cause celebre* amongst the English public as feelings of sympathy for the passengers grew in proportion to the outrage at the treatment they had received at the hands of Degraves. There were visits to the *Hope* by noteworthy public figures from parliament and also the church. One of these was Joseph Butterworth, the member for Dover and a close friend and supporter of William Wilberforce. He visited the Wesleyans aboard the *Hope* to assess the situation himself and was ultimately pivotal in providing a solution to the *impasse*. There were also sympathetic newspaper articles, both in England and in Van Diemen's Land, warning potential emigrants to be very wary when booking a passage else they end up in a similar situation.[128] Support for the *Hope's* passengers also took more practical forms such as assistance with their day-to-day material needs, which were becoming critical as the ship became infested with rats that ate into their meagre reserves of food. As news of the passengers' plight spread, Wesleyan congregations from across England contributed to their welfare with food and other needs. And while the passengers worked for some resolution to their problem, the ship's owners had problems of their own. Macintosh had been imprisoned in Dover

---

[128] It is certain that Mary Reibey would have heard of the events taking place in Ramsgate and, as Macintosh's name was mentioned, it would have probably adversely effected her opinion of him.

Castle whilst Degraves had somehow managed to gain release and was lobbying various influential people for a resolution to the dispute on his own terms.

Eventually the deadlock was broken when Butterworth convinced Parliament to charter a vessel, the *Heroine*, to take the *Hope's* passengers to Hobart where they eventually arrived toward the end of 1822, without ever getting their money back from Degraves. [129] Meanwhile, at Royal Ramsgate Harbour, Lloyds had agreed to repair the damaged *Hope* and the old ship underwent extensive repairs and some considerable improvement, including the expensive renewal of her copper sheathing. Whether it had always been Degraves' intention to create a situation whereby Lloyds would pay for the repairs and renovations that the *Hope* badly needed is impossible to determine. Robert Mather and other passengers claimed that he had always intended to either wreck the ship or run it aground and then claim the insurance money. While such a scheme seems unlikely at first glance, there is a body of evidence that supports the idea, for Degraves and Macintosh had insured the ship for about £3,000 which was close to double what she had cost them. [130]

Whatever his original plans, Degraves was ever an extraordinarily adaptable opportunist. In his insurance claim to Lloyds he argued that the *Hope* had been extensively damaged by the storm; whilst to the Lords of Admiralty and Lord Bathurst he claimed that the laying of the ship on the ground at Ramsgate after her seizure by Customs caused considerable

---

[129]The Wesleyan's final voyage to Van Diemen's Land aboard the *Heroine* is in itself a fascinating tale but not within the scope of this work. Of equal interest is the impact on Tasmanian society of many of the *Hope's* original passengers but again this is not within the scope of this work.

[130] In his letter to Lord Bathurst dated 18th December 1822 Degraves states that they had insured the Hope for £2,000; in the *London Times* report of 5th March 1823 trial it was stated the Hope was insured for £3,000.

additional damage and further, that customs officers had dropped overboard some small boxes containing very expensive machinery components, for all of which he demanded £7,000 compensation from the government on top of the Lloyds insurance money. Whilst these claims were disputed by both the passengers and the Ramsgate Port Authorities (the passengers claimed that the *Hope* was already in a poor state of repair when it left London), Degraves and Macintosh's financial position was improved greatly, for even though they did not get the full £7,000 claimed they still managed to secure £2,000 from Treasury for the supposed losses caused by Customs and a significant payment from Lloyds. They also retained the passengers' fare monies.

Despite these financial windfalls, Degraves was not content. He saw another opportunity for a substantial gain by bringing a suit for libel against the proprietors of the *London Courier*. Degraves, who was a prolific litigant, claimed that he and Macintosh had been seriously slandered by the *London Courier's* article of January 1822 and that the newspaper, which sympathetically described the plight of the emigrants on board the *Hope*, had cost them both income and reputation. He sued for £10,000 for libel on the basis that the newspaper's claim, that Degraves and Macintosh had been using the *Hope* to orchestrate an insurance scam, was false. To put the sum claimed into perspective, it represented approximately 300 years' wages for a semi-skilled worker in the 1820s, or enough money to buy three brand new ships of around the *Hope's* size.

The libel hearing took place before a judge and jury on 5th March 1823 and, after hearing conflicting evidence from a large number of witnesses, the judge advised the jury that on a technical point the proprietors of the *London Courier* were, in law, guilty of libel. The jury's response was to award Degraves and Macintosh a trifling £300 in damages, while the judge did not award Degraves costs. Indeed the damages awarded was such a small amount that it could reasonably be taken as a calculated insult and was a clear indication that the jury's sympathies lay with the newspaper publishers, for £300 would not have even covered Degraves' legal costs.

The court action against the *London Courier* and the criminal charges for breech of the Passengers Act were not the only court cases in which Degraves was engaged prior to his departure. From the letters he later wrote from Hobart gaol it is clear that he had a considerable number of other cases running in various courts around London, in some of which he was the plaintiff and in others he was the defendant. The potential consequences of the latter appear to have been substantially greater than the former which was why Degraves was clearly so anxious to depart for distant shores. On 19th September 1823 the, now thoroughly renovated, *Hope* finally left England with Degraves and Macintosh aboard, this time well before the beginning of the storm season.[131] Before leaving England Macintosh took out another insurance policy with Lloyds and again Macintosh is listed as the sole owner of the *Hope*.[132]

---

[131] *Hobart Town Gazette* 1st April 1824. p. 2

[132] The Lloyds Registers from 1800 to 1820 show that *Hope* was built in Bristol of English oak in 1793. However, when the *Hope* sailed out of English waters in 1823 she was registered with Lloyd's as a ship built in Venice. This (possibly deliberate) error regarding the *Hope's* origins was repeated in all following Lloyds registers and is still present in modern maritime history books where the *Hope* is mentioned such as in Ronald Parson's comprehensive book *Shipping Losses and Casualties in Australia and New Zealand,* which even states that the *Hope* was an American built ship.

177

Chapter Thirteen: From Ramsgate Harbour to Hobart Town

In Autumn 1823 the renovated *Hope* headed down the English Channel then sailed south and west past the Lizard and Land's End. From there Macintosh and Degraves took the normal zigzag route to Australia sailing south-west across the Atlantic to Rio De Janeiro where they took on fresh supplies. They then sailed east and south to catch the trade winds back across the Atlantic to Cape Town where they remained for some time. On the 18th February 1824 she set sail on the last leg for Hobart Town arriving in early April 1824. In total the voyage took seven months, almost double the normal time.

When the *Hope* left England she was under the command of a new master, Captain Ansell. Ansell, like Captain Allison, seems not to have maintained good relations with the *Hope's* owners and was soon replaced by a Captain S. Kormack in Cape Town, which might account for the delay there. Captain Ansell was not the only person on board the *Hope* who left the ship at Cape Town; William Macintosh also decided that he had had enough of his Uncle Peter Degraves. William disembarked in Cape Town and from there took a ship to Madras where his other Degraves uncle, now a Lt. Colonel, lived. His plan was to join the Madras army as a cadet as his father had done. Henry Degraves was doing quite well for himself in Madras, still in the army he had progressed his fortune tolerably well and now owned a large home in Wallajabad, a small town to the south west of Madras. Henry Degraves shared his home with a " native woman" whose name was Ammi and with whom he had a daughter who was a little younger than William Macintosh.

No doubt it was difficult for Macintosh to bid farewell to his son, now a young man, who he had hoped he would share his new life with in Hobart.

Still, to Hobart he was committed regardless of the antics of his brother-in-law and the revolving door of the ship's Captains. According to the Lloyd's register Captain Kormack remained in command of the *Hope* until she was sold at the beginning of 1826 however, just as the ownership and origins of the *Hope* were obscured by Degraves, so too, it seems, was the identity of her Master. Contrary to information in the Lloyds records, local Australian newspapers such as the *Sydney Gazette* and the Hobart based *Colonial Times* continually stated in their "Shipping News" sections that the master of the *Hope* was a Captain Norris. Norris is even noted as being the master of the *Hope* when she arrived in Hobart for the first time in April 1824 with Degraves and Macintosh on board. It is an indication of Degraves' well documented abrasive nature that there were three different captains on the *Hope* for the one trip from England to Hobart.

It is also interesting to note that the *Sydney Gazette* stated that when the *Hope* arrived in Hobart she carried a total of 43 passengers, including Mr and Mrs Degraves, their eight children and Hugh Macintosh. This was less than half the 92 passengers who had originally been crammed on board when the *Hope* set sail on her first, abortive, attempt to reach Van Diemen's Land in 1821.

Once the *Hope* had docked in Hobart the Degraves family and their cargo were unloaded at the wharf on Hunter's Island, which had only recently been connected to the mainland by a stone causeway which later became Hunter's Street. Interestingly Macintosh (who now called himself Major Macintosh) did not disembark with his sister and brother-in-law but stayed on board the *Hope,* and immediately set sail for Sydney to deliver goods and passengers there. It can be reasonably assumed that Macintosh was fed up with being in the company of Peter Degraves and was travelling to Sydney to renew his acquaintance with Mary Reibey. Indeed there is significant evidence to suggest he did exactly that; for on the *Hope's* first journey out of Sydney a few weeks later she carried freight belonging to Mary Reibey.

Macintosh stayed in Sydney until October then returned to Hobart. What was he doing for those five months? One has to assume that he and Mary Reibey were exploring the possibilities of their relationship. There is no doubt that a strong affection had developed between Macintosh and Mary Reibey in the months they spent together in London however the time spent apart was now a factor, three years had elapsed since their time in London.

Figure 42: Mary Reibey's Sydney house on George Street, which was handy to the Sydney docks and her warehouses. Would Macintosh have stayed at her house for the five months that he spent in Sydney or in a nearby hotel?

Also working against Macintosh was the fact that the colonial newspapers had given extensive coverage to the debacle involving the *Hope* and the Wesleyans in Ramsgate. The effect of this coverage was magnified because Mary and her fellow passengers had also been scammed by the dishonest owner of the *Mariner*, being forced to re-victual the ship at their own expense when food supplies ran out only a few weeks into the journey from London to Sydney. This must have affected her opinion of Macintosh and there can be little doubt that Macintosh would have tried to convince her that these things were all in the hands of Degraves and that he had no idea of what was going on, which was probably true. In the end Macintosh stayed in Sydney five months but returned to Hobart without the committed affections of Mary Reibey.

Not all Macintosh's time in Sydney was spent trying to rebuild his relationship with Mary Reibey, he was also learning from her; for there were other, more pragmatic, aspects to their relationship. Mary's business interests were extensive and, as well as rural properties, hotels and warehouses, she also owned ships, some of which undertook sealing operations in the Bass Strait whilst others ran the trade routes in Asia. So with Mary's guidance Macintosh quickly came to understand how the colonial traders were making their fortunes. As a result Macintosh purchased goods for the *Hope* to carry into the Asian trade routes so that in early June 1824, after only a few weeks in Sydney Harbour the *Hope* set sail on a trading circuit through Asia. The *Hope* carried fur seal skins brought to Sydney by the sealers from Bass Strait and the Southern Ocean and other goods that were now being produced by the young colony. Fully laden the *Hope* made first for China (the usual ports of call there were either Hong Kong or Macau), where the seal skins in particular were in high demand from the wealthy Chinese and could bring huge profits. Then from China the *Hope* carried on trading or carrying freight between various Asian ports before arriving at the Isle of France (Mauritius) where she took on a cargo of "3,000 bags of sugar, 260 cases of wine, 30 casks of treacle..." and of course rum, all for Sydney where she arrived in the last days of December 1824 after a passage of 45 days. The profits from this trading run would have gone some way to rebuilding Macintosh's fortunes for the early 1820's was a time of chronic shortage of ships in the Australian colonies and it was clearly the intention of Macintosh to use the *Hope* as a means of increasing his capital by completing and returning to the Asian trade circuit as frequently as possible, which was exactly what occurred.

While Macintosh was in Sydney and the *Hope* was sailing the trading routes of Asia, Degraves was busy building their saw mill. He immediately saw that the most efficient way to power the mill was by water, rather than by steam as he had originally intended. Having surveyed the streams descending from Mount Wellington above Hobart, Degraves determined the best site for his mill was at a place called the Cascade on the Hobart Rivulet, which lay just inside a block of land owned by a Mr. Robert Murray, a settler who had arrived in Hobart in 1821. Not deterred that someone else already owned the perfect site for his sawmill Degraves did not approach the owner of the land to negotiate some mutually beneficial arrangement, instead he applied for a grant of the adjoining 2,000 acre block, which took in the heavily timbered slopes of Mount Wellington (part of which is still owned by the Cascade Brewery today) but which did not include the Cascade itself. Here began the first of numerous controversies in which Degraves would embroil himself in his new home.

Never one to let the possibility of a dispute over a technicality stand in the way of his plans, Degraves then bribed a government surveyor to re-surveyed the land he had been granted and together they moved the boundary a little to the south and west so as to include the Cascade site in his land grant rather than that of his neighbour. So with the use of a pencil and a rubber and a little bribery Degraves gained the land where now the Cascade Brewery stands. By the time his neighbour Robert Murray discovered the ruse, construction of the saw mill was well under way. Murray launched legal proceedings and a battle that lasted years followed, during which Degraves simply protested his innocence and continued as if he owned the land

and while the matter was before the courts he built and began operating in succession the saw mill, the flour mill and the brewery. Degraves initially appealed to Lieutenant Governor Arthur to have the matter thrown out of court, but Arthur sided with the original owner. Then, when Degraves appealed to Governor Brisbane in Sydney, Arthur advised Governor Brisbane that the case amounted to nothing more than a "most glaring land job" by Degraves. Never one to be easily put off and ever the eager litigant, Degraves continued his case in the Courts where he accused his neighbour Robert Murray of every kind of deception. The Court ultimately found in favour of Murray. When Justice Pedder gave his verdict in 1832, the mills had been supplying much-needed sawn timber and flour to Hobart Town for nearly seven years. Neither the colonial administration nor the court would have wanted to interrupt such an important activity and Pedder's judgement, therefore, merely required Degraves to pay Murray £300 for the land he had usurped. While this was a substantial sum it was an outcome that would have suited Degraves well enough, for he had achieved his desire of owning the Cascade site. Nevertheless it did his reputation, already tarnished in Hobart by the *Hope* episode, no good at all, for the Wesleyans had arrived in Hobart nearly three years before Degraves so everyone had already heard, first hand, how he had mistreated them.

Shortly after work began on the sawmill Degraves attempted to convince Lieutenant Governor Arthur that he should be given a contract to supply Hobart Town with reticulated water, an idea that was clearly a revamp of his plans for the Isle of Lewis. In the meanwhile Macintosh had returned from Sydney and, within a short time he purchased a substantial agricultural property on the fertile northern bank of the Derwent River between Bridgewater and New Norfolk, directly opposite land granted to Lt. Governor Arthur and beneath the towering rugged slopes of Mount Dromedary.

Macintosh called his new home "Lawn Farm" and, with convict labour to do the hard work, he set about fulfilling his dream of establishing a landed estate, growing Bordeaux grapevines, fruit trees and raising merino sheep and Yorkshire cattle.

Indeed his merinos thrived at Lawn Farm, where the combination of fertile river flats and the dry rocky slopes of Mount Dromedary suited his sheep so well that they soon won the Merino Society's prize for the finest wool. On Lawn Farm the wine grapes and fruit trees also thrived and it may well be that Hugh Macintosh was actually Tasmania's first wine maker.

Early in 1825 Macintosh's son William arrived in Hobart. He was now a young man of eighteen, come to visit his father and cousins in Hobart. William had decided not to follow his father's path into the military; rather he would try a career in business. Hugh had written William glowing reports of their progress in Hobart and encouraged him to visit to see how he liked the life there. William left Calcutta with a friend of his father's, Major Suetonius Todd, who was also sailing to Hobart on Macintosh's advice. The widowed Todd was visiting Macintosh to meet the single sister-in-law of his neighbour at Lawn Farm, Mary Macdonald, whose family had sailed out on the *Hope*. William stayed long enough in Hobart to be certain that he did not find the life there to his liking and, by early 1825 William was writing to friends in Madras, making plans to return to India and take up a commercial cadetship in the East India Company.

Meanwhile Major Todd and Mary Macdonald had married and, with Todd's furlough coming to an end, they booked passage back to Calcutta on the ship *Medina* leaving on the 21st October 1825. The newly weds were travelling cabin class and William convinced his father that it was a good idea that he should return to Calcutta in the company of Major and Mrs Todd on board the *Medina* to follow his dream of making his fortune in India.

Figure 43: The native eucalyptus trees grew straight and tall on the slopes of Mount Wellington above Hobart Town. When Macintosh and Degraves arrived sawing in sawpits, such as the one shown above, was how most timber was cut. Macintosh and Degraves' saw mill changed that and enabled the growing colony a steady supply of sawn timber, freeing labour for other tasks.

By early 1825 the Macintosh and Degraves sawmill was in operation producing good quality sawn timber for the builders of the rapidly expanding Hobart Town. Immediately the sawmill became operational Degraves turned his attention to making a flour mill using the steam engine he had original intended for the saw mill. After some consideration however he instead used the simple and more reliable power of the rivulet to drive the flour mill's grindstones.

Figure 44: The Cascade Mill's water wheel designed and built by Peter Degraves to power the wood saws and flour mills at Cascade Mill

All in all things were going very well for the partnership of Macintosh and Degraves until suddenly, at the end of 1825, Peter Degraves' past caught up with him. Those people to whom he owed money in London had tracked him to Hobart and, using a local agent, instigated legal proceedings against him. Interestingly the man heading the group of Degraves' creditors in the legal proceedings was a Mister Bishop, who was in fact Hugh Macintosh's uncle (brother of his mother). Bishop was also the guardian of the daughter of one of Macintosh's close friends who was a British military advisor still stationed in Persia. Typically, when Degraves' creditors' agents filed the necessary papers with the Hobart Court, Degraves refused to acknowledge the debts and began a series of complicated legal arguments designed to convince the courts and the government of his innocence. After a series of short trials in May 1826 Degraves was arrested and imprisoned for non-payment of his London debts. From prison he continued to proclaim the unjustness of his imprisonment and wrote innumerable letters and memorials, all of which contained elaborate falsehoods, to every person of influence within his reach however his efforts were in vain and he remained in prison for five years.

Figure 45: Governor Arthur; formerly a Royal Army general he was a governor in Honduras, Van Diemen's Land and Canada.

Meanwhile Macintosh acted quickly to protect his own assets and also the assets of the Macintosh & Degraves partnership from court proceedings against Degraves. In October and November 1826 he advertised in the *Hobart Town Gazette* that the partnership of Macintosh and Degraves was dissolved by mutual consent and that all that firm's debts would be paid by Hugh Macintosh. [133] This was a well planned and necessary manoeuvre to insulate Macintosh from Degraves' debts and also to prevent the saw mill being seized by Degraves' creditors. The final settlement date offered by Macintosh for the payment of these debts was mid November 1826. After settling the partnership's debts the mill and machinery at the Cascade became the sole property of Hugh Macintosh who then ensured that the Cascade's employees understood that whilst he was now in sole control of the mills he was placing his two eldest nephews, Henry and Charles Degraves, in charge of the day to day operation of the mill. Once he was certain that the affairs in Hobart were settled Macintosh sailed to Sydney, where he organised the sale of the *Hope* to the local firm of Askwith & Co. a little before the end of 1826. Up until her sale the *Hope* had continued to operate out of Sydney, plying the Asian trade routes and carrying a range of trade goods, almost always including some belonging to Mary Reibey. With the money from the sale of the *Hope* as well as the proceeds from her successful trading runs plus the remaining cash he still held Macintosh would have been comfortably positioned financially. More importantly he was also free of the risk of being caught up in the legal maelstrom engulfing Peter Degraves.

After the sale of the *Hope*, Macintosh disappeared from the Australian colonies for almost two years. There is no mention of

---

[133] It is important to note that this advertisement referred to the debts of the partnership incurred in Hobart i.e. the partnership of the Macintosh and Degraves Saw Mills. Macintosh was not accepting any responsibility for any of Degraves' personal debts.

his presence in any of the Sydney or Hobart newspapers other than a notice which appears in the *Hobart Town Gazette* on the 6th October 1827 in which his name appears on a list of unclaimed letters awaiting collection at the Hobart Post Office. As it was the practice for these letters to be advertised after they had been left unclaimed for three months it is a clear indication Macintosh was no longer in the colony.

Macintosh returned to Hobart on the ship *Wanstead* on the 18th May 1828. The *Wanstead* had sailed from London on the 2nd December 1827 and stopped at the usual places on route. There are two likely explanations for Macintosh's leaving Australia, one may have been to try to get Peter Degraves out of jail by finding some remedy in England for those financial problems that kept him imprisoned in Hobart; the other may have been to chase the general's half-pay pension he had been promised by the Shah of Persia but which had not been paid to him for some time.

Because of the extensive delays in correspondence between Britain and Hobart any written negotiations towards a settlement between aggrieved parties could drag on for years with the delay between a letter written and a reply received often taking in excess of 12 months. This was highly undesirable if one party, like Degraves, happened to be languishing in jail. The only way to short circuit this process was to have a trusted third party travel back to Britain to handle negotiations with Degraves' creditors face to face. It is certain that Lt. Colonel Henry Degraves was also involved in this process because, in September 1827, Henry guaranteed by bond to "… repay £263 2s 6d to Charles Jones, Dover, Kent, Gentleman." Charles Jones was Peter Degraves' uncle, the brother of his mother. As the amount to be repaid was the same amount that Peter Degraves had charged (and not repaid) Robert Mather for a cabin and his

Figure 46: Hobart Town, from Bellerive, as it looked during the times of Macintosh and Degraves. Historic records tell us that in the 19th century Mount Wellington carried snow for almost 80% of the year. The Cascade is located at the base of the V shaped central valley above.

passage on the *Hope* in 1821 it seems certain that there must have been a connection between Mather and Jones though what it was we do not know. We do know that Charles Jones was a successful business man who had taken over the family transport business in Dover and who had seen Peter Degraves regularly wheedle money from his widowed sister Deborah Decharme. Charles Jones had also seen his sister Deborah committed to an asylum for the insane as a result of the debacle of the *Hope's* seizure at Ramsgate and the public shame brought about by the extensive media coverage of that event. Further Charles Jones had seen his other sister, Anne Degraves, Peter Degraves' mother, die broken hearted as a consequence of the Ramsgate events only a few weeks after Deborah was placed in the asylum. There can be little doubt that that Charles Jones, Peter Degraves' uncle, despised his nephew for why else would he have pursued him to Hobart and there have him imprisoned for five long years? It is indeed interesting that both Macintosh's and Degraves' uncles were involved in the case that put Degraves in prison.

Unfortunately for his brother-in-law Macintosh's efforts in England did not result in Degraves release and the latter remained in jail for another three years after Macintosh's return from the British Isles, on the *Wanstead*, in 1828.

Having disembarked in Hobart on the 18th of May 1828 Macintosh went immediately to the home of his sister Sophia, which was only a short walk from Hunter's Wharf. Sophia Degraves had moved from her home at the Cascade and was living with her younger children in a well appointed brick cottage at Wellington Bridge only a short walk from Hobart's jail in Bathurst Street, where she visited her husband every day. Sophia also supplemented her income by teaching.

The location of her cottage was also convenient to the general store run by the Jewish convict brothers Judah and Joseph Solomon who were responsible for the building of Hobart's first and only synagogue.[134] Once he arrived at Sophia's cottage Macintosh spent some time explaining to his sister the outcomes of his endeavours overseas as well as giving her other news from 'home'. The following day he visited Degraves in prison and informed him of what he might now expect from the law suits against him. When his business with the Degraves was complete Macintosh went to inspect the operations at the Cascade saw mill and was pleased to find that the production of sawn timber was now between nine to ten thousand feet each week. While staying at the Cascades he wrote a memorial to Lt.

---

[134] Wellington Bridge was situated near the corner of Elizabeth and Liverpool Streets, about where the National Bank now stands. There is some evidence that Sophia was able to afford to rent this house and support her eight children through the support of Henry Degraves and Macintosh.

Gov. Arthur requesting a personal grant of land of 2,000 acres, additional to the 2,000 acres granted to Degraves on the slopes of Mount Wellington.[135] Once his memorial to the Lt. Governor had been delivered Macintosh travelled up the Derwent River to his sanctuary at Lawn Farm, perhaps wondering at the irony of life that his business was located on the slopes of a mountain named after the General he had fought for so often in India and on the edge of a city named after the father of the man who had placed him in Persia.

There is little historic material that sheds light on Macintosh's life through the period from his return to Hobart in 1828 to his death in 1834 although one thing that we do know, from land deeds held in Hobart, is that he was intent on expanding his pastoral ambitions. After 1828 he added to his agricultural holdings at Lawn Farm by purchasing a further 2,000 acres on the Esk River and another 2,000 acres on the Elizabeth River. Both these blocks were prime grazing country. The purchase of these blocks made Major Macintosh one of Tasmania's largest landowners at that time.

Apart from his agricultural pursuits we know that one of Macintosh's most important contributions to Australia's cultural history also occurred in this period.

Peter Degraves, whilst in prison, became close friends with a well educated and eloquent young Englishman named Henry Savery, a fellow inmate who, like Degraves, was imprisoned for debt. Savery, under Macintosh's direct patronage, would write Australia's first novel, *Quintus Servington*.[136]

---

[135] This was granted posthumously in 1836; for the benefit of Macintosh's son William.

[136] Now also known as *The Bitter Bread of Banishment*.

Henry Savery was the sixth son of the wealthy Bristol banker John Savery. He was well educated, receiving a classical and commercial education. Henry was a highly intelligent and charming young man with an extensive circle of friends in the highest levels of British society. Despite the opportunity to do so he did not follow his father into what he saw as the boring profession of banking, attempting instead a more entrepreneurial path that combined the editorship of the newspaper *The Bristol Observer* with running an insurance brokerage and a sugar refining business. When all three businesses failed Savery was faced with financial ruin and in an attempt to rescue his fortunes he resorted to forgery, illegally procuring over £40,000 (about three million dollars in today's money) between 1822 and 1824. He was arrested in late 1824 on board a ship trying to flee England for America. When confronted with his crimes and the fact that death by hanging was by far the most likely sentence, Savery appears to have had a nervous breakdown and attempted to commit suicide by throwing himself overboard. He remained on the verge of insanity for some time. In 1825 he was sentenced to death by hanging; yet despite the vast amounts of money involved Savery (like Degraves) had friends in powerful places. The day before he was due to be executed, he learned that his sentence had been commuted to transportation for life.

Once in Hobart his high level of education, his personal charms and his skills in book keeping, meant that he soon attained a privileged position working in the offices of the colonial administration and so spent the first years of his sentence in relative comfort. However Henry's preference for the 'high life' and living beyond his means was a habit that died hard and to service his growing debts he began forging promissory notes, which were, at that time, in common use in Hobart because of a shortage of hard cash.

Around this time he was also writing to his wife, Eliza, assuring her that he was doing well in Hobart, trying to convince her to come out to be with him. Early in 1828 Eliza Savery sailed from England in the *Jessie Lawson*, but nearly lost her life when that ship was wrecked. After being rescued she continued on in the ship *Henry Wellesley* (named after Arthur Wellesley's younger brother) and arrived at Hobart in October only to find Savery was still bonded and being threatened with a writ for debt. Savery's distress at his wife finding him in such a situation was heightened by rumours that she had been having an extramarital relationship with Algernon Montagu, Hobart's new attorney-general, into whose care Eliza's parents had entrusted her on the voyage.

Shortly after his wife's arrival in Hobart Savery's forgeries were discovered and he was arrested for fraud. The combination of personal and financial pressures pushed Savery over the edge once more and he attempted suicide by cutting his throat with a razor but was saved by the well known Hobart surgeon Dr William Crowther.

When he had recovered from his self inflicted wounds Savery went to trial and in December 1828 he found himself in Hobart's prison where he met Peter Degraves, a man with whom he had much in common. Both were well educated, had a wealth of personal charm, were highly intelligent and were happy to bend the truth if it suited them. Interestingly both were also prolific litigants. No doubt they found considerable comfort in conversation during their mutual confinement. Meanwhile, with her husband imprisoned and his dubious reputation in utter ruins, Eliza Savery left Hobart in mid-February 1829, and never returned.

In March 1830, when Savery came due for what we might now call parole, Degraves was still in prison but he wrote to the Colonial Secretary, who was well acquainted with both Savery and Degraves, requesting that Savery (still a convict) be assigned to Major Macintosh at Lawn Farm. The government agreed to the request and Savery was released into Macintosh's care, but with a stipulation which showed that Governor Arthur had a clear understanding of the weaknesses in Savery's character:

> If Savory (sic) be discharged from Jail, I wish him to be assigned to Major Macintosh with the positive condition that he is to reside at his Farm in the neighbourhood of New Norfolk and is not to be allowed to Trade or be employed on his own account in any way.

It is likely Savery and Macintosh knew each other before Savery was imprisoned as Hobart's society was small, so classically educated persons from similar well-to-do backgrounds such as Savery and Macintosh would certainly have met. This is reinforced by the fact that Macintosh essentially invited Savery into his home, direct from jail, and almost immediately made him the overseer of his farm.[137] Also, although Savery was 15 years Macintosh's junior and a convicted criminal, they would have been considered social equals. Certainly Macintosh respected and supported Savery's need and desire to write, for he allowed him the time and energy to write *Quintus Servington* and a number of essays while he was living at Lawn Farm.

Interestingly Savery showed again the restless nature of his multi-facetted mind and did not engage himself only in writing while he lived under Macintosh's roof. At Lawn farm his

---

[137] Indeed it would seem that the pair formed a close friendship for even after Macintosh's death Savery continued to live at, and manage, Lawn Farm until he once more fell into debt and once more attempted to solve his money problems by making forged notes. He was arrest and reimprisoned at Port Arthur in 1840, sentenced by his wife's ex-lover the Attorney General Montagu. He died at Port Arthur in 1842, possibly by suicide.

intellect seems to have become fascinated by the challenges of agriculture as he assisted Macintosh with the development of the property. Savery became quite enthusiastic in his embrace, study and application of agricultural principles, to the point where, in November 1834, he wrote to Governor Arthur (whose own farm was opposite Lawn Farm across the Derwent River) giving him detailed advice on what might be done to improve his fields.

In late 1831, when Peter Degraves was finally released from prison, because of the work Macintosh and his two nephews had done, the saw mill and flour mill at the Cascade were both thriving. Immediately Degraves was released Macintosh revived the partnership of Macintosh and Degraves Saw Mills and put the day to day operations of the mills back into the hands of Peter Degraves. Early in 1832 work was begun on building the Cascade's first brewery and by the end of that year The Cascade Brewery was producing "genuine beer from malt and hops, either in a cask or bottle, and of very superior quality." Thus it was that when the traveller and journalist, Edward Markham, visited the Cascade, in 1833, the Macintosh / Degraves partnership had already added to their milling operations with the brewery, as well as a brick kiln, a lime kiln, a laboratory and they were also breeding and selling yeast to bakers. On top of that they were well advanced in the process of more than doubling the size of the family home at the Cascade.

Sadly, even as the Cascade's mills and new brewery flourished, the worsening condition of Macintosh's war wounds meant that he now required almost constant medical attention, obliging him to spend almost all of his time in Hobart. When Edward Markham met Macintosh at the Degraves' home, he recorded that:

> … Major Macintosh, who I believe, at the Mutiny of the Madras Army, led his regiment against the King's troops. This was in the time of Sir George Barlow. He, of course,

after the thing was quitted, left the Service and was many years in the Persian Service teaching them the European tactics etc. Major Macintosh always lives with the Degraves and is considered the first. He has been severely wounded and is a good scholar. He teaches the young Degraves Latin etc.

As Markham noted the ailing Macintosh now stayed with the Degraves family at the Cascade, close to the medical service available in Hobart and where he was able to enjoy the company of his young nieces and nephews who he not only instructed in Latin and Greek but also taught to play a variety of musical instruments including both the violin and the much rarer and difficult nail violin.[138] His beloved Lawn Farm was left in the care of Henry Savery who, with the added prestige and responsibility, became even more engrossed in studying the latest advances in agriculture and applying them to Macintosh's farm.[139]

Toward the end of 1833 it became clear to Macintosh that the remaining days of his life might now be measured in months rather than years so he sent word to his son William, who was in India, to come to him. After a sea journey that took a couple of months to complete, on the 8th September 1834 William Macintosh, in the company of his cousin Charles Degraves, arrived in Hobart aboard the ship *Merope* from Mauritius. It is very likely that William Macintosh also brought his father news of the death of his friend Abbas Mirza in October of 1833, aged only 44. Then three months after William's arrival in Hobart, on the 22nd of December 1834, another ship arrived from India bringing news that Peter Degraves' brother, Lieutenant Colonel

---

[138] A Wilson *Degraves Family History* p.54

[139] After Macintosh's death Henry Savoury once more fell into debt and once again forged bills. He was arrested, and in October 1840 was condemned by his wife's former lover, Montagu, and sent to Port Arthur, where he died, possibly from a stroke, on 6 February 1842

Henry Degraves, had died on the 3rd September 1834 in his home at Wallajahbad in India. For Peter Degraves it was the loss of a brother he had not seen for many years and had, in fact, never spent much time with; for Hugh Macintosh it was the death of a dear friend and brother officer who had shared with him the high adventure of his youth; the horrors and joys, the losses and victories, the intensity of bloody battles and the monotony of long dusty marches.[140] News of the death of Henry Degraves must have been a blow to Hugh Macintosh for only two days later he was dead, dieing peacefully at the Cascade in the home of his sister and brother-in-law, surrounded by his family and the beginnings of the business empire that would not have come into existence without him.

Christmas eve of 1834 was indeed a strangely sorrowful day for the family living at the Cascade with the news of Henry Degraves' death so suddenly followed by the death of Hugh Macintosh and all falling together on the 24th of December 1834, which was Peter Degraves' 56th birthday.

---

[140] Henry Degraves' will still exists in the British Library. It shows that he left his home and all his worldly possessions to be divided equally between his Indian wife and their daughter.

Chapter Fourteen: The Degraves' Empire

Figure 47: Whilst this painting of the Cascade Brewery and Mill by Haughton Forrest was done around 1880 all the buildings shown had been built by the time of Peter Degraves' death in 1854.

After Macintosh's death Peter Degraves assumed sole control of the Cascade's businesses. Hooper and other of Degraves' biographers state that Macintosh left Degraves his share of the business and also a 2,000 acre land grant on the Elizabeth River in his will. However this is obviously an incorrect assumption by these historians as Macintosh's will has not survived and Hooper *et al* did not know of William Macintosh's existence. It is more likely, as William was present at his father's death, that Degraves purchased or came to some other arrangement to acquire William's share in the Cascade's business. As the fate of William Macintosh is not known other than that he returned to India in 1835 it is unlikely that the nature of their arrangement will ever be known, although some of Degraves' actions immediately after William Macintosh left the colony are interesting.

Within a few months of William Macintosh sailing for India Peter Degraves wrote to the Lt. Governor purporting to be William Macintosh's 'attorney' and asked that the 2000 acre land grant on the Elizabeth River, which had been tentatively granted to Hugh Macintosh in 1828, be confirmed; and after a flurry of persuasive letters by Degraves this was accomplished. But did William ever end up as the owner of the land? No; the 2,000 acres of prime land along the banks of the Elizabeth River ended up belonging to Peter Degraves.

Peter Degraves (probably for the first time in his adult life) was now finally free from debt so, with a solid infrastructure in place, the Cascade businesses flourished, though not without Degraves managing to generate more conflict and controversy in the small society of Hobart Town.

While arguing with the authorities over Macintosh's 2,000 acres on the Elizabeth River, Degraves added a new flour mill to his operations at the Cascade; the new mill was powered by a revolutionary, highly efficient water turbine of French design that generated over 60 horsepower. To meet the water demands of the expanded milling and brewing operations Degraves decided to dam the Hobart Rivulet above the Cascade to guarantee a reliable water supply for his mills. The problem was that the rivulet's water was also the main water supply for the people of Hobart so Degraves' dam immediately antagonised the population who suddenly found themselves without water as the rivulet's flow decreased to a trickle. Naturally the citizens complained to the government and the issue came to a violent head when, in 1835, Hobart's Town Surveyor put Degraves on notice to stop damming the rivulet. Of course Degraves ignored the request and refused to release the water so the government sent a party of eighteen constables to open the dam's sluice gate. The story goes that Peter Degraves blocked the party of constables' access to dam by threatening them with a pick axe handle, or some similar length of heavy timber. Eventually the constables overpowered the indignant Degraves and tore open the dam's sluice gates. This action gave only temporary relief and Hobart Town's water supply remained a contentious subject until once more, in 1845, Degraves temporarily cut off the water and caused another public outcry, which made Degraves even more enemies in Hobart. Then in 1848 John Moore, editor of the *Hobart Town Guardian*, used that newspaper to accuse Degraves of conspiring with the newly appointed Lt. Governor Denison to revisit the issue of Cascade's water rights to the detriment of Hobart's citizens. Degraves responded by threatening Moore, promising to hire a couple of thugs to beat him up. Moore considered the threat genuine so immediately laid charges that resulted in Degraves being issued a summons to answer the charges in court. Of course Degraves ignored the summons so he was arrested and imprisoned until he agreed to sign a bond to keep the peace.

During this period of zealous expansion in the 1830's Degraves also became involved in the movement to construct a theatre for Hobart, now the Theatre Royal, which is still considered one of the best theatres in Australia for acoustics as well as being Australia's oldest, still operational, theatre. The theatre's syndicate opened to public subscription in 1837 and many of Hobart's business and cultural elite pledged or contributed towards the cost of what was then expected to become the hub of the town's cultural life. Degraves subscribed to the building fund after which his eldest son, Henry, tendered for the contract to design and build the theatre, Degraves famously presented himself as a fully qualified architect, although it is now clear that he was not.

Henry Degraves won the contract to build the theatre but soon, true to form, his father began arguing with the other parties involved in the project and quickly fell out with the syndicate members claiming that they owed him (or his son) over £2,000 toward the cost of the building.

Figure 48: Interior view of Hobart's Theatre Royal, built by Henry Degraves and probably designed by his father. The Theatre Royal is Australia's oldest theatre and is still, essentially, as Peter Degraves designed it. Its is generally agreed the Theatre Royal has the best acoustics of any Australian theatre.

As the disputes increased work on the theatre ground to a halt. Degraves then tried his renowned negotiating skills on some of the subscribers to buy out their shares at a discount. Most were not interested in selling, particularly to Degraves. To resolve the stalemate the theatre was put up for public auction in 1839, Degraves was the highest bidder and became the sole proprietor.

The Theatre Royal remained a possession of the Degraves family until after Peter Degraves death. Interestingly local legend has it that he never attended a single event at the theatre. This raises the interesting question of who was actually behind the culturally disinterested Degraves' involvement in building the Theatre Royal? Like all of Degraves' versions of his own history that have been handed down, the Theatre Royal was all Peter Degraves' idea however, it was actually his son Henry who was responsible for the building of the theatre: the same Henry who had learned to paint and play the violin from his Uncle Hugh Macintosh. Indeed it is highly likely that the more cultured, classically educated Sophia Degraves and her sons were the driving force behind Degraves' uncharacteristic cultural endeavour; this is reinforced by the fact that Degraves complained that it was his worst ever investment, never returning him more than three percent!

At the same time as the Theatre Royal was under construction the Degraves family was also thinking of going into ship building and so applied for a grant of waterfront land near the Mulgrave Battery. However it was not until 1841 that they received a suitable lease, near the end of Castray Esplanade at Battery Point. As with the theatre, history tells us that the ship building was a venture initiated by Peter Degraves however it was actually his son Henry who owned the business. Among the ships built by Henry Degraves were the barque *Lady Emma* (203 tons), and the schooners *Miranda* (127 tons), *Fair Tasmanian* (145 tons) and *Jenny Lind* (136 tons). In 1847 he built the barque *Tasman* (563 tons), said to be the largest sailing ship ever built in Van Diemen's Land. The schooner *Circassian* (105 tons), the brig *Yarra* (139 tons) and the barque *Melbourne* (150 tons) were built in 1851. The shipyard was closed when the gold rush began in Victoria due to the lack of skilled workers, they all having rushed off to the gold fields. Despite the closing of the ship building yards the Degraves ships, loaded with timber, flour, beer and other supplies for the growing town of Melbourne, sailed out of Hobart in a steady stream that continued to increase the Degraves family fortune.

After a protracted illness, Sophia Degraves died in Hobart in May 1842, aged 53. Following her death Peter Degraves focused on his businesses until his own death at the Cascades on the 31st of December 1852, aged 74, probably dying with some satisfaction knowing that he was now reckoned to be what he had always pretended to be; an wealthy and powerful member of society, not just in Hobart but across all the Australian colonies.

Figure 49: Peter's eldest son Henry Degraves, the builder of Hobart's Theatre Royal, Australia's oldest operational theatre; Henry Degraves also built ships, including Tasmania's largest sailing ship, the *Tasman*.

In his will Degraves provided well for all his children but left his business empire in the control of his eldest son Henry who, only two years later, died suddenly at the age of forty three, leaving no heirs. Control of the family business then passed to Henry's three brothers. Of these only John and Charles remained involved in the family businesses in Hobart however neither men married and so produced no legitimate children. Degraves' youngest son, William, born in 1820, moved to Port Phillip where he became a wealthy merchant, flour miller and pastoralist. From 1860 until 1874 he was a member of the Victorian Legislative Council. He married in 1850 and died in Hobart in 1883 without issue. Interestingly William Degraves was used as a model for a "... narrow-minded, irascible... self made man" by the 19th century novelist Jessie Couvreur (Tasma) who had come into close contact with William Degraves when her husband managed properties owned by him.[141]

At this point in the story it is worth mentioning that, according to one Australian family's traditions, the Degraves' male line did not end in the 19th century but continued through an illegitimate child fathered either by Peter or his son William, in 1850, by a young servant girl who worked in the family home at the Cascade. At the request of Degraves, one of their workers, named John Howard, married the pregnant 18 year old and raised the child as his own however the name William Degraves was included as the first and middle name for subsequent males of that line for several generations.

Tragically two of Peter Degraves' daughters, his eldest, Louisa Davis along with her husband and four children, and his fourth daughter, Ellen Fenwick, and her four children, all drowned in the catastrophic wreck of the *Royal Charter* which was smashed to pieces on the rocks of the north coast of Anglesey, Wales in

---

[141] P. Clancy 'Tasma: A Woman Novelist of Colonial Men and 'Continental' Men' *Explorations,* No. 30; University of Melbourne.

1859 during what was generally described as the worst hurricane of the 19th century. Local traditions have it that Degraves' son-in-law, the husband of Ellen Fenwick, who had remained in Hobart, killed himself when he heard of the loss of his wife and children.

Figure 50: Peter and Sophia's second youngest daughter, Deborah Hope Degraves, was born in August 1821 in London while the *Hope* was being readied to leave for Hobart. Deborah later married Sir James Wilson and was the only one of Degraves' eight children to produce a surviving line of (legitimate) descendants.

Another of Peter Degraves' daughters, Sophia, died of typhoid in Florence, Italy.

His only surviving daughter Deborah Hope Degraves married James Wilson who was a friend of her brother William Degraves. Not long after the death of her brother, Henry Degraves, James Wilson took over the day to day management of the Cascade brewery. Wilson also, later, became Premier of Tasmania (1869-72). Deborah and James Wilson had five children all of whom ultimately returned to live out their days in Britain.

So it was that, even though Peter and Sophia Degraves had produced nine children including four sons, the Degraves name had disappeared entirely from Tasmania before the end of the 19th century. However the business empire Hugh Macintosh and Peter Degraves built and the history that Degraves had fabricated for posterity would survive a great deal longer.

Conclusion: The Advantages of a Deceptive Distance

The stories of Peter Degraves and Hugh Macintosh reveal two very different men who lived very different lives but were brought together by family connections and the possibilities offered by a new life in Hobart Town. Macintosh had capital but as an "officer and a gentleman" he had no interest in being a businessman, rather he aspired to use his capital to create a life for himself as one of the colony's landed gentry. Degraves had plenty of ideas and business experience, but had a ruined reputation and no cash. As such, each needed the assistance of the other to take full advantage of the inducements offered by the British government to encourage "men of capital" to move to Australia. The result of their union was the creation of the most enduring feature of Tasmania's economic landscape, the Cascade Brewery.

As individuals each man was also directly responsible for two of the oldest, still existent, features in Australia's cultural landscape. Macintosh, by supporting Henry Savery and allowing him both the time and place in which to write, was responsible for Australia's first novel while Degraves was (indirectly) responsible for the creation of Australia's oldest still operational theatre, Hobart's Theatre Royal. Despite this, and their equal contributions in the founding of the Cascade's business empire, history has treated these two very differently: Macintosh's life has been largely ignored whilst Degraves' has been well documented, albeit inaccurately.

To a degree the treatment of these men's lives is a reflection of the differences in the men themselves, while also being an indication of the biases that often exist within the processes of recording and disseminating history. Whilst my examination of the histories of Hugh Macintosh and Peter Degraves has revealed much of what was previously unknown about the two men, as well as correcting various inaccuracies, it has not dealt directly with the question of why there has been such a pronounced discrepancy between the assumptions within the popular histories of these men and the archival record.

The results of this work clearly demonstrate that the public view of Macintosh and Degraves has been shaped by how information has been placed within the public domain, over time, by various public and private institutions and how readily historians are prepared to accept the "historical status quo" by relying of those readily accessible myths created by Peter Degraves for the information from which they constructed their histories. The institution primarily responsible for the dissemination of the histories of these two men has been the Cascade Brewery. In the 20th century Cascade published two 'histories', *A Page from the Past, the Cascade Brewery: the Degraves' Centenary 1824-1924* (1924) and *Cascades: a Taste of History* (1991). Both 'histories' obliquely used the Degraves' story and its deep connections to Tasmanian history as a marketing tool to enhance the brand's image, reputation and products as well as to increase access to the tourism market. Cascade Brewery, in its creation of these histories, has, perhaps ironically, perpetuated the mythology that Peter Degraves himself created around his own life, helping him to complete the reinvention of his personal history while ignoring the more interesting life of Hugh Macintosh. (It is my hope that one of the results of this work will be that the contributions of Hugh Macintosh will feature more prominently in the historical narratives that the Cascade Brewery produces in the future.)

One of the primary factors that protected Degraves' version of his life, during his lifetime and after, was the "tyranny of distance". Degraves exploited the inadequacy of long distance communication between social and geographic centres to manipulate his history. Prior to the advent of the digitalisation of many archival collections around the world and their ready accessibility through search engines such as Google, the distance that separated the scattered fragments of information needed to re-assemble Degraves' real life story ensured his falsehoods avoided detection.

However once the various pieces of Degraves' life were assembled it became possible to understand why he fabricated so many aspects of his past, for it was surely a habit that began early in his life, after he, his brother and mother were abandoned by Dr. Degravers. Ashamed of his father's behaviour and desperate to raise his social standing Peter Degraves, some time before the age of 20, began to subtly manipulate his history. He removed the 'r' to turn Degravers into Degraves; he implied that his father had died rather than run away; he exaggerated his father's professional and social status. This propensity for playing with the truth grew as the physical and chronological distance from his past increased. By the time Degraves had established himself in Hobart, where he hoped, not only for financial success, but to be finally accepted as a member of the "upper classes", the truth of his life had become very bent indeed. By the time of Hugh Macintosh's death on Christmas Eve, 1834, almost everything to do with Degraves' public version of his life prior to his arrival in Van Diemen's Land was either a gross exaggeration or a complete fabrication.

The use of distance by Hugh Macintosh was considerably different from that of his brother-in-law, for the only chapter of his life that he might have been inclined to obscure was the Madras 'White Mutiny' but that had been so thoroughly documented in the contemporary British press that his role in it was well known, so he made no attempt to hide it. Rather, it can be argued, Macintosh used distance as a means for solving problems in his life. Macintosh's motives are harder to divine than those of Degraves because we do not know who his parents were. It was the general practice of the British upper classes that the wealth of an estate would pass to the eldest son and, commonly, the second son would build a career in the military as did Macintosh with his choice of a vocation in distant India at age fourteen.[142] Later, when he could not find a wife in India, he solved the problem by returning to England. Then, after the trauma of his court martial in 1810, unable to follow his career path in the British military, he used distance to continue his career in Persia where his skills and experience would not be retarded by the effects of his involvement in the mutiny. When he returned to Britain from Persia with insufficient capital to enable him to live the lifestyle he desired, he used distance again, the move to Hobart, to progress to the next phase of his life where he could put the capital he had accumulated to work more effectively.

The lives of Hugh Macintosh and Peter Degraves demonstrate how the "tyranny of distance", whether between the colonies and the homeland or between cities and towns within Britain, created a situation wherein the personal histories of individuals could be deliberately hidden, obscured, ignored or falsified. Examples of this are found in the story of Arthur Orton, a butcher from Wagga who successfully impersonated the dead Baronet Roger Tichborne for almost a decade, deceiving even Tichborne's elderly mother. Or the case of Jonathon Hugo who, in 1811, convinced the commandant of Launceston, Lieutenant-Colonel Gordon that he was a "prince of the Royal Blood". Both of these men created these false identities to gain financial and social advantage.

Perhaps the most infamous colonial impostor was the accomplished identity thief, John Dow, an ex-convict who, in New South Wales, in 1833-34, successfully posed as Viscount Lascelles, the son of the Earl of Harewood. Dow spent months running up huge bills on credit and even married the daughter of

---

[142] While the vocational choice was probably strongly influenced by his parents Macintosh would still have seen the solution to the problem being solved by him moving to a distant land.

the owner of one of the hotels in which he resided. John Dow, like Degraves, seems to have come to believe his own fabrications.

However the issues raised through the study of Peter Degraves belong to a different tradition of impostors; persons from a respectable backgrounds who, on arrival in the colonies inflated, exaggerated, invented or glossed over aspects of their past in order to gain a degree of social prestige or financial advantage that would have been difficult or impossible to achieve in Britain. Such falsification of one's social connections, credentials or status was essentially snobbery and was commonly used in both Britain and Australia in order to gain social advantages, though there was a growing trend in Australian society to view such endeavours with distain as is shown in the below piece from the 1857 *Melbourne Punch*.

Colonial Snobbery
Many circumstances of late years have encouraged the supposition that snobbery was on the wane; but it ever and anon breaks out in a fresh place... Snobbery, like thistles and Scotchmen, thrives anywhere. It must, else how could it have taken root in a new country such as ours... and often self-entitled dignitaries as are to be found.

Yet it was the distain that the upper classes, in both Britain and Australia, felt for people who had risen from humble beginnings to wealth gained in "trade" which created the social barriers that Degraves had, for most of his life, tried desperately to break through and which, upon his arrival in Hobart, he finally succeeded in doing.

To achieve his dream Degraves had to hide his apprenticeship with Railton and Ranking and his failed and insignificant cotton mill. Instead of being a bankrupt travelling salesman he was "... first in the firm of two country banks ... and principle Capitalist of a considerable Mercantile house in the city of London" who owned a vastly successful string of mills that employed thousands of people. With this false description of his past Degraves portrayed himself as a wealthy capitalist rather than the struggling speculator he actually was and any failure that beset him was the fault of Napoleon or some other dubious character. In the colonies in the 1820's such reinvention was crucial for gaining access to land, cheap labour and government contracts as well as those social connections that could also bring social and economic benefit. Such snobbery contrasted strongly with the beginnings of the, so called, egalitarian Australian society inferred in the *Melbourne Punch* article, wherein people were to be judged on their present merits rather than their past errors and the adoption of the traditional British class system was generally abhorred, as was demonstrated by the overwhelming public resistance to Wentworth's attempt to set up a "Bunyip Aristocracy" in the late 1830's. Mary Reibey and other ex-convicts or their children (such as Wentworth), who progressed to become valuable members of society are good examples of this and they stand in stark contrast to people, such as Degraves, who fabricated the magnitude of their past achievements and social stature in order to impress colonial peers.

Yet despite his faults and falsehoods there can be no denying the actual brilliance of Peter Degraves' mind and size of his achievements during the thirty odd years he lived in Hobart Town. Although he was not an architect he designed and built numerous substantial and impressive buildings that still stand today. Although he was neither an engineer or a miller or a brewer he designed, built and operated mills, breweries and such; whilst in 1847 his shipyards built the largest sailing ship ever built in Tasmania.

Hugh Macintosh leaves a very different impression: he was a man who had seen and done so much that he would have had a right to brag about his achievements and would have been welcomed in the highest levels of Society. He had begun his life at one of Britain's most exclusive schools and had the social connections that Degraves only dreamed of. He had met the Shah of Persia and was and intimate friend of the Persian Crown Prince. He had travelled the length and breadth of India in the company of Britain's most celebrated military hero, the Duke of Wellington, leading his troops into some of Britain's most bloody and important battles of the period. And yet, until the publication of this work, he was almost historically invisible for he did not promote himself or seek social acclaim.

Crimes of Mobility

Peter Degraves and his father were early examples of what have been described as "crimes of mobility" wherein individuals, so inclined, were able to take advantage of the increased mobility, both social and geographical, that was a feature of the 19th century. In his work on this subject criminologist Dr L. Friedman maintains that the more mobile a society becomes the easier it is for a person to create a false identity and then use that identity to exploit a situation or person for financial or some other form of advantage. Interestingly the crime of bigamy, particularly for financial advantage (such as committed by Dr Degravers in Edinburgh) is singled out by Friedman as the "crime of mobility" that most proliferated in the 19th century, followed by falsification of one's social status or professional qualifications, such as was carried out by Peter Degraves.

However unlike his father, who was without a doubt a bigamist and a quack, Peter Degraves was, somewhat like the famous modern impostor Frank Abagnale Jr. (brought to public attention by Leonardo Decaprio in the film *Catch Me If You Can*), not only able to convince his peers that his false qualifications were real but could produce results as if he had the actual qualifications he claimed. [143] Whether he managed this by employing people who were suitably qualified or whether, as this work suggests, this was the result of his actual genius may never be known. Regardless of which is the case Peter Degraves can certainly be regarded as Tasmania's most successful liar.

Unlike his brother-in-law Peter Degraves, Hugh Macintosh does not seem to have shown any desire to promote himself socially. It appears he was content to remain quietly at the Cascade with his nephews and nieces teaching them to paint or play the violin or to speak Latin and Greek while enjoying the peaceful life at Lawn Farm on the banks of the Derwent River. A thorough search of Hobart's newspapers, journals and other contemporary material in the public domain from the period 1824 to 1834 did not reveal any mention of Macintosh attending any social gatherings in Hobart. Rather it seems that he consciously avoided the social whirl of Hobart where, with his exotic military background, he would most likely have been feted.

Hugh Macintosh and Peter Degraves were very different men who, together, left an indelible mark on Tasmanian and Australian history and it is testimony to Degraves' success in fabricating his history that he finally gained the social standing he sought, though in the process he probably made more enemies than friends. And it is a testimony to the saying "The victor writes the history." that those who later wrote of him appear to have unconditionally believed his stories.

Postscript
In completing this work I am ultimately left with the feeling of its incompleteness, this is not because of any serious inadequacy in the general information about Macintosh or Degraves

---

[143] F. Abagnale Jr. *Catch Me If You Can* (New York) 2002. Abagnale assumed eight separate identities and successfully impersonated, for extended periods, an airline pilot, a senior doctor and a lawyer.

themselves but by the frustration of not being able to offer more than a tiny glimpse of the women in their lives. In the case of Degraves we have several women who were pivotal in his life but of whom there is no known historic record. Firstly there is his mother, Anne Jones, who supported Degraves and his brother after their father deserted them but who died of a broken heart after the debacle surrounding the seizure of the *Hope* at Ramsgate. Then there is Degraves' aunt, Deborah Decharme, who financed Degraves' early entrepreneurial activities; then acted for him when he was bankrupt and lent him money for the expedition to Hobart only to be driven to insanity by the deceptions practiced on her by her nephew. Lastly Sophia Macintosh, a woman who not only bore and raised his nine children but, like so many 19th century women, loyally followed her husband around Britain and, eventually, to the very ends of the earth, where as a cultured and intelligent woman she felt isolated and lonely. While Peter Degraves was five years in prison in Hobart Sophia somehow supported her large family as well as her husband. In her own way Sophia Degraves was as much responsible for the success of the Cascade's businesses as her brother and her husband yet there is almost nothing recorded of her life. Similarly there exists almost nothing of the short but fascinating life of Mary Macintosh (nee: Nicholson), a young woman who mixed with some of the most interesting, forward thinking people of her time and who also helped raise the young Mary Shelley. Though her life was short we can but wonder at the spirit of a young woman prepared to leave England for life in a hill fort high on the Mysore plateau. The only other woman we know of to feature in Hugh Macintosh's life was Mary Reibey, well known in her time and famous in the 20th and 21st centuries as the face on the Australian \$20 note, yet except for the scant records of her few surviving letters and a short journal the details of this famous Australian woman's life are virtually unknown. The reality is that the full story of the lives of prominent men in history, such as Macintosh and Degraves, cannot be fully understood without some corresponding knowledge of the stories of the women with whom they shared their lives and dreams.

Appendix 1: The Wreck of the Hope and the Bruny Island Treasure

The Wreck of the Colonial ship *Hope*.

A Short History of Bruny Island's Buried Treasure Mystery
It was a dark and stormy night on the 29th of April 1827 when the colonial trading ship *Hope* was shipwrecked on the beach which now bears its name at South Arm near the mouth of the Derwent River, Hobart Town Tasmania. With the shipwreck of the *Hope* one of Australia's greatest treasure mysteries began, the Lost Treasure of Bruny Island. Since that time in history many people have visited Bruny Island searching for the treasure. Below is an exact reprint of the shipwreck of the *Hope* from the newspaper *"The Colonial Times"* May 1827. As well as accurately describing the event of the loss of the ship this news piece gives a good feel for the horror of a shipwreck in the early 19th Century.

From the Hobart *Colonial Times* May 1827

The Loss of the Hope
We have the painful duty to report the loss of the barque *Hope*, which vessel was wrecked on Sunday morning last, on the long Sandy Beach, between Betsy and Iron-pot Islands. It appears she was on her way from Sydney hither, with about 100 tons of freight, and the following passengers: Ensign Barcley, 40th Regiment; Mrs. Bisbee and Mr. Bisbee (wife and brother of Mr. Bisbee of Hobart Town who came as passengers in the ship Elizabeth from England to Sydney); also Mrs. Westbrook mother of Dr. Westbrook. Of this place, another passenger per the Elizabeth, and three others, among whom is Mr. Edmund Johnson, nephew of Mr. Joseph Johnson of the Green Ponds.

The *Hope* made the Heads on Saturday afternoon; and took on board, off Cape Raoul, the pilot, Mr. Mansfield, the same evening, shortly before dusk. The *Hope* at this time was being towed in by two of the ship's boats; but the pilot having taken charge of the vessel, told Captain Cunningham, that he could safely bring her up the river, without the assistance of the boats; from which, in consequence, she parted.

The Captain, however, wished the vessel might be towed in; but the Pilot observed, that his long experience in the river Derwent would enable him to bring her up in safety otherwise. The Captain was perfectly aware of sufficient room being afforded in the Derwent for any vessel to be brought up with almost any wind, and therefore acquiesced with the Pilot's wishes; and, leaving the charge of the vessel in his hands, retired to rest, where he remained until awakened by the vessel running on shore.

The wind light and variable, and the vessel proceeded up the river but slowly. The night was rather dark and rainy; and about 4 o'clock on the morning of Sunday; about two hours before day break, she, by some means, we can scarcely conceive how, ran ashore, on the long sandy beach, in Shoal Bay, as above stated.

Although the night was rather dark, the wind was not violent, but the surf was running tremendously high. On the lead line being thrown, she was discovered to be in seven feet of water, while her proper draught was fifteen. The moment she struck, the consternation and terror became general; and the scene is described as truly terrific.

The Captain raving at the pilot like a man distracted, the latter standing in mute dismay--- females just left their beds--- sailors not knowing which way to turn, to relieve the creaking vessel, which was expected to go to pieces every moment, as she already leaked like a sieve--- the heavy surf rolling over her, adding horror to the scene--- while the dismal half hour guns of distress seemed to signal the death knell of all on board. Daylight at length appeared and discovered to the sufferers their truly perilous situation.

About 10 o'clock of the Sunday morning, two whale-boats, of Mr. Lucus's fishing party, which had been laying off Bruny Island, came up to the wreck. They had heard the proceeding evening the signal-gun for the Pilot, which drew their attention and induced them to bend their steps thitherward.

They immediately lent their aid, with the ship's jolly boat, in getting out the ship's bower and kedge anchors; but the attempt proved fruitless, for one of the whaleboats (the property of Mr. Kelly), was stove, having her head absolutely dashed off, and the crew narrowly escaped with their lives. Captain Cunningham then jumped into the jolly boat alone, which parted from the other boat, and nearly fell a sacrifice to his eager promptitude, to save the vessel. Finding every other hope lost, to all the lives they could became their chief object.

The venerable Mrs. Westbrook and Mrs. Bisbee were safely conveyed on shore, after a state of most dreadful suspense for four hours. All this time, the rolling of the vessel almost precluded anyone from keeping their feet, while the state of the two females was most dreadful; overcome with weakness and terror, and fatigue, they could not stand without support, which was kindly afforded by a Mr. John Elliot and some other Gentlemen passengers. With the Ladies, Mr. Clarkson, charterer of the *Hope*, came up to Hobart Town by the whale-boat in the course of Sunday, bringing the fatal news to Town, leaving the other persons on board. Immediately on learning the fate of the *Hope*, the Agent (Mr. Behune), dispatched the sloop *Recovery*, a small craft, in order to bring away a portion of her cargo, in which she succeeded, having returned the following evening with as many tons of goods as could be thrown on board from the wreck.

But to return to the ship. On Sunday night, between 11 and 12 o'clock, the rudder gave way, and the upper part of her stern was driven in. At this critical hour of the night, it was every moment feared that the stern post would give way or be driven in also; in which case the vessel must soon afterwards have foundered, and every soul on board perished as the surf was still running mountains high. The other passengers who did not come up on Sunday safely arrived in Town on Tuesday- till which period all hands were employed at the pumps, in imminent peril, every moment in danger of being washed overboard. When some Gentlemen who left the wreck on Tuesday, who had visited it on Monday, the sea was gaining on the vessel every hour, her main mast had been cut away, and all hopes of saving her were given up. Some casks of spirits, which were on board, were ascertained to have been damaged by the salt water; and the tea and sugar, which also formed part of her cargo, must inevitably be destroyed. We understand, that among the persons who had merchandise on board is Mr. James Lord, owner of the *Marquis of Lausdown*.---- We are not aware whether the vessel is insured or not.

The government brig *Prince Leopold*, in coming from Maria Island with the remainder of the wreck of the Apollo, saw the *Hope* off the Heads on Saturday, and safely arrived in the Harbour the same evening. Monday she discharged her lading, and on Tuesday was immediately sent to the relief of the wrecked *Hope*.

(End: *Colonial Times* report)

As mentioned in the historic account above the shipwreck of the *Hope* occurred on a beach on the north side of the entrance to the mouth of the Derwent River on South Arm, directly opposite Bruny Island and its historic Kelly's Point (now known as Dennes Point).

The shipwreck of the *Hope* marked a turning point in the history of Bruny Island and Hobart Town as it prompted a number of changes to the government's policies to navigation around the mouth of the Derwent River including the construction of a navigation light, and then a lighthouse, on Iron Pot Island to accurately define the entrance to the Derwent River.

The history of the *Hope* and her lost treasure has become interwoven with the history of Bruny Island, in fact the treasure has become known as the "Bruny Island Treasure" and mention of it pops up in most history books concerned with Bruny Island's history or Australian treasure legends.

You will have noticed that, whilst the history of the shipwreck is covered in some detail in the newspaper article above, there is no mention of a treasure being on board or of a treasure being lost or a treasure on Bruny Island. The reason for this is probably due to the fact that the oral histories associated with this legend report that the treasure was the Hobart garrison's (40th Regiment) quarterly pay and Hobart's military government would have had numerous reasons for keeping the loss of the garrison's pay a secret. Certainly there is no reference to the pay's loss in official histories from that time. To find out more about the treasure we have to fast forward from 1827 to the 1850's when the whaling stations on Kelly's Point had gone and the Denne family had acquired most of the northern tip of Bruny Island and built a beautiful mansion overlooking the Channel and Storm Bay.

In about 1856 a mysterious Irishman, named McKinnon, turned up on Bruny Island at Denne's Point, directly across Storm Bay from where the *Hope* was wrecked. Fortunately for Bruny Island history noted maritime historian Captain Harry O'May recorded the recollection of this event, and those that followed, by Bruny Island's long lived resident Darcy Denne in his book "*Shipwrecks of Tasmania*". Darcy Denne lived well into his 90's and actually met and came to know quite well the mysterious McKinnon. Below is an extract from Harry O'May's book.

"It was said to be the pay money for the garrison stationed in Hobart Town. At the time of the wreck the treasure disappeared. The two soldiers were suspected of securing it and secretly hiding it in the sand dunes with the intention of retrieving it later. This was never possible as the men were transferred to India where one of them died. The other returned to England where he received his discharge. Probably he had no means of returning to Hobart Town. However, this man told his story to an Irish farmer named McKinnon and convinced him that the buried treasure was still to be found where he and his mate had planted it. McKinnon sold his farm and, with a rough plan of the locality supplied by the ex-soldier, came out to Hobart Town. There he purchased tools and stores, obtained a miner's right and engaged Donald McKay, owner of the passage boat Mary May, to land him and his gear, not on Hope Beach, but on Kelly's Point on Bruny Island. Hope Beach and Kelly's Point are on opposite sides of the entrance to the Derwent and approximately three miles of open water separates them.
On the arrival of the Mary May at Kelly's Point, Mr. Harry Denne came down to the jetty and assisted in the landing

of the gear. This included a large and very heavy box which cost the three men considerable effort to place on the wharf.

After the boat had gone on her way Mr. Denne questioned the stranger but received only evasive answers. He became a man of mystery to the Dennes who watched him as he tramped aimlessly about the shore. Next morning he was still there but the heavy metal box was gone from the jetty. During the day he was asked why he was prying around and he answered, "I am searching for hone stones." (Stones used for sharpening cutting tools.)

The Dennes decided this was a very unsatisfactory answer and that it was time to communicate with the police. The Brown's River trooper was instructed to investigate the case. When the trooper asked why the stranger was prospecting on private property he was also told of the search for honing stones. The trooper then asked, "What is in the big box?" and was told it contained snake-bite cure. When it was opened two small phials of some liquid were found in the box.

The trooper had no excuse for arresting the man who continued his prospecting for some time and then disappeared.

But after a lapse of 18 months he turned up again. It was learned later that in the meantime he had returned to Ireland and secured from the soldier another map with more minute instructions. On his return to Hobart Town, McKinnon arranged with Captain Bill Whisby of the ketch Ann Allen to convey him to Bligh's Point which is about a mile further up the Channel. He told Whisby for what he was hunting and this time he gave all the gullies in the vicinity a thorough combing before he abandoned the search. When all his money was gone he returned to Hobart Town and worked as a labourer."

The hunt for the *Hope's* lost treasure continued for many years, with sometimes large parties of men digging here and there about Nebraska Beach and nearby gullies. In 1946 a supposed map of the treasure's location turned up in Hobart and a syndicate was formed that employed men and machinery to dig a large area over a period of several weeks but no treasure was ever found... or was it? Some locals maintain that the treasure has been found but that the finder kept quiet about it.

Bibliography

Primary Sources

Allen T.   *A History of the County of Surrey* (London) 1831
Atkinson W.   *Liberal Education of the 19th Century*, (New York)
1878
Beatson A.   *A View of the Origin and Conduct of the War with
                Tippoo Sultan*, (London) 1800
Benson-Walker S *Reminiscences of the Life (*Hobart) 1884
Blakiston C.   *Twelve Years' Military Adventure* (London) 1829
Boulger D.   *England and Russia in Central Asia*, Vol. 2
                (London) 1879
Bowering L.   *Haidar Ali and Tipu Sultan* (London) 1893
Carpenter W.   *Peerage for the People* (London) 1841

Campbell L. Ed.   *The Asiatic Annual Register* (Calcutta) 1807

Campbell J.   *Reports of Cases Determined in the Courts of Kings
                Bench* (London) 1811
Degravers P.   *A Complete Physico-Medical and Chirurgical
                Treatise on the Human Eye.* (New York) 1992
Dodwell E.   *Alphabetical list of Officers of the Indian Army*
                (London) 1839
Falconbridge A. *An Account of the Slave Trade on the Coast of Africa*
                (London) 1788
Fularton A.   *The Topographical and Historical Gazetteer of
                Scotland.* Vol. 1 (Edinburgh) 1853
Gray F.   *Recollections of North Bruny Island* (Hobart) 1978
Hipkins F.   *Repton School Register 1620-1894* (London) 1895
Hookham   *The Critical Review* Ed. T. Smollett (London) 1794
Kay J.   *A Series of Original Portraits and Caricatures with
                Biographical Sketches and Illustrative Anecdotes*
                (Edinburgh) 1838

Leary G.	*Lives of great and celebrated characters of all ages* (New York) 1860
Lloyd G.	*Thirty Three Years in Tasmania and Victoria* (London) 1862
Malcolm J.	*A History of Persia Vol. 2* (London) 1829
Markham, E	*Voyage to Van Dieman's Land, aboard the ship Warrior 17th March 1833 to 7th February 1834*(from original held at Mitchell Library Sydney).
Morris E.	*Cassell's Picturesque Australasia* (London) 1889
Nicholson W.	*The Life of William Nicholson,* (Oxford) 1868
Ouseley W.	*Travels in Various Counties of the East* (London) 1819
Ross C.(Ed)	*Correspondence of Charles 1st Marquis of Cornwallis* (London) 1859
Thorn, W.	*Memoir of the War in India Conducted by General Lord Lake, Commander in Chief, and Major General Sir Arthur Wellesley; from its commencement in 1803 to its termination in 1806* (London) 1818,

Archival Material

British National Archives: Item details HO 47/45/3
British National Archives *Lancaster Assizes 1810* HO 47/45/3
PRO, Chancery Masters Exhibits C/107/7 *J.P Degravers to James Rogers.*
British Library India Collection, Item 5. L.AG.23.10.1
British Library Asia Collection N/2/4/48
British Library Asia Collection N/2/3/17
British Library India Office Records Reference: Z/O/1/10 No. 6357
British Library Collections, India office; Degravers, Henry ref. IOR/L/MIL/9/255/151v
British Library Collections, *The India Office and Burma Office List: 1824*
British Library India Office Records L/MIL/9/110/ f.268
British Library, *The Madras Military Fund* L.AG.23.10.1
Tasmanian State Archives, *Letter from Peter Degraves to Arthur,* CSO 1/234/5665
Tasmanian State Archives, *Bonwick Transcripts,* Box 13, pp. 6259>6279

Tasmanian State Archives, CSO SC292/1/1
Tasmania State Archives, *CSO* 1/229/5619
Tasmanian State Archives, *Wayne Index* 'McI'
Tasmanian State Archives, CSO1/1/154/3714
Tasmanian State Archives, CSO 1/8/117
University of Tasmania Archives, M10/1 up to and including M10/12

Letters and Memorials

Arthur to Bathurst *Historic Records of Australia* Vol. 2 p. 566
H.R.H. Duke of York to Lord Cornwallis 26 July 1788 (E. Thompson *Rise and Fulfilment of British Rule in India* 1962 p.175)
Lord Cornwallis to H.R.H. Duke of York 12 August 1787 (in E. Thompson *Rise and Fulfilment of British Rule in India* 1962 p.174)
National Archives of Scotland: *'Letters of P. Degraves 1819'* Seaforth Muniments GD46/17/51
Degraves to Bathurst 18 December 1822 Bonwick Transcripts: Box 13, p. 6275 Tasmanian State Archives
Degraves to Arthur 5 August 1828; CSO/1/154/3714
Degraves to Frankland 6 January 1836 CSO 1/281/6767
Degraves to the Colonial Secretary 6 July 1836 CSO 1/281/6767
Memorial of Hugh Macintosh to the H.E.I.C. 13 October 1821 Utas Archives M10/7
Memorial of Macintosh to Lt. Gov. Arthur 1 May 1828, CSO 1/281/6767
Macintosh to Bathurst 20 June 1821 C.O. 201/106 'M'
Macintosh to Bathurst 6 September, 1821 C.O. 201/106 'M'
Macintosh and Degraves to Lord Bathurst 18 Dec. 1822 Bonwick Papers Vol. 3 pp. 6248-6287

Contemporary Newspapers and Journals

Australian

Hobart Town Gazette 20 May 1822
Hobart Town Gazette 1 April 1824.
Hobart Town Gazette 22 October 1825
Hobart Town Gazette 21 May 1828

Colonial Times 31 March 1825
Colonial Times 16 February 1827
Sydney Gazette 6 May 1824
Sydney Gazette 31 March 1825
Sydney Gazette 22 September 1825
Sydney Gazette 22 September 1825
Sydney Gazette 31 March 1825
Sydney Gazette 13 March 1825
Melbourne Punch 22 January, 1857

British

Public Advertiser 5 July 1780
Morning Chronicle and London Advertiser 7 July 1780
London Courant and Westminster Chronicle 11 July 1780
Gazetteer and New daily Advertiser 18 Sept. 1780
Caledonian Mercury 20 January 1787
London Gazette, 1805 to 1810
Aberdeen Times 7 February 1810
The Gentleman's Magazine Vol. 119 Jan. 1816 'Memoir of the Late Mr. W. Nicholson'
London Courier 3 January 1822
London Times 6 March 1823
Oriental Herald 1827
Journal of the Royal Asiatic Society of Great Britain & Ireland, Vol. 16, 1856
The Oxford Journal 1869
English Law Reports 1903
Edinburgh Medical Journal 1905

Secondary Sources

Books

Abagnale F.   *Catch Me If You Can* (New York) 2002
Alexander A. *The Companion to Tasmanian History* (Hobart) 2005
Allen D.   *Clive's Lost Treasure* (London) 1978

Allport C.   *A page from the past, the Cascade Brewery: the Degraves' centenary 1824-1924* (Hobart) 1924

Baker S.   *The Ship* (London) 2002

Bailey H.(ed.)   *Cambridge History of Iran* (Cambridge) 1991

Bathurst B.   *The Wreckers* (London) 2005

Bennett B.   *Mary Wollstonecraft Shelley: an introduction.* (London) 1998

Bingham M.   *Cascade: A Taste of History* (Hobart) 1991

Blaikie G.   *Scandals of Australia's Strange Past* (Adelaide) 1963

Blainey G.   *The Tyranny of Distance* (Melbourne) 1966

Blackburn T.   *A miscellany of mutinies and massacres in India* (Delhi) 2007

Bowden K.   *Capt. James Kelly of Hobart Town* (Melbourne) 1964

Braithwaite A   *A Guide-book to Kirkby Stephen,* (London) 1922

Broadbent J.   *India, China, Australia* (Sydney) 2003

Cardew A.   *The White Mutiny* (Bombay) 1929

Charley, C.   *Hunting for Treasure* (London) 1990

Cooper R.   *The Anglo-Maratha Campaigns and the Contest for India* (Cambridge) 2003

Davis, B.   *A Guide to Bruny Island History* (Hobart) 1990

Diene D.   *From Chains to Bonds* (London) 2001

Denning G.   *Mr Bligh's Bad language* (Cambridge) 1992

Edney M.   *Mapping an Empire: the geographical construction of British India* (London) 1990

Ellis V.   *Louisa Anne Meredith: a tigress in exile.* (Hobart) 1979

Eyre W.   *The East India Company* (New York) 1945

Gabriel T.   *Hindu-Muslim Relations in North Malabar* (New York) 1996

Gardam, J.   *A History of Brown's River* (Kingston) 1988

Giblin R.   *The Early History of Tasmania* (Melbourne) 1928

Gibson J.   *Deacon Brodie: Father to Jekyll and Hyde* (Edinburgh) 1993

Gibson A.   *Prices, food and Wages in Scotland 1550 to 1780* (London) 1995

Grant R.   *Representations of British emigration, Colonisation and Settlement* (New York) 2005
Hadgraft C.Ed.   *The Bitter Bread of Banishment* (Sydney) 1984
Hainsworth D.   *The Sydney Traders* (Melbourne) 1981
Hartwell R.   *The economic development of Van Diemen's Land, 1820-1850* (Melbourne) 1953.
Henderson, G.   *Maritime Archaeology in Australia* (Perth) 1986
Hirst J.   *Sense and Nonsense in Australian History* (Melbourne) 2005
Hobsbawm E.   'Inventing Traditions' *The Invention of Traditions* ed. E. Hobsbawm (Cambridge) 1983
Irvine N   *Dear Cousin: The Reibey Letters* (Sydney) 1995
Jones W.   *Prosperity Robinson, the life of Viscount Goderich* (New York) 1967
Kerr, G.   *The Tasmanian Trading Ketch* (Portland) 1987
Lock S.   *The Oxford Illustrated Companion to Medicine* (Oxford) 2001
Madgwick R.   *Immigration into Eastern Australia 1788-1851* (London) 1937
MacMillan D   *Scotland and Australia 1788 to 1850* (Oxford) 1967
McNeice R.   *Coins and Tokens of Tasmania, 1803-1910* (Hobart) 1969
Maxwell-Stewart H.   'Land of Sorrow; Land of Honey' in P & A Elias, eds. *A Few from Afar* (Hobart) 2003
McKenzie K.   *Scandal in the Colonies* (Sydney) 2004
McKenzie K.   *A Swindler's Progress* (Sydney) 2010
McWilliam R   *The Tichborne Claimant* (London) 2007

Millar J.   *True Australian Sea Stories* (Sydney) 1978

Mukherjee R.   *The Rise and Fall of the East India Company* (Berlin)
Norman L.   *Pioneer Shipping of Tasmania* (Hobart) 1938
O'May D   *Ferries of the Derwent* (Hobart) 1988
O'May H   *Wrecks in Tasmanian Waters* (Hobart) 1954
Parkin R   *H.M. Bark Endeavour* (Melbourne) 1997
Parsons R.   *Shipping Losses and Casualties in Australia and New Zealand* (Adelaide) 2003
Philips C.H.   *The East India Company 1784-1834* (London) 1940
Prentis M.   *The Scots in Australia* (Sydney) 1983

232

Rickard S. *Lifelines from Calcutta* (Sydney) 2003

Richards W *"Her Majesty's army, Indian and colonial forces: a descriptive account of the various regiments now comprising the Queen's forces in India and the colonies"* (London) 1891

Roe M. *Quest for Authority in Eastern Australia 1835-51* (London)

Simpson E. *The Robert Louis Stevenson Originals* (London) 2005

Sardesai G. *New History of the Marathas Vol. 3* (Bombay) 1948

Sherington G. *Australia's Immigrants 1788-1978* (Sydney) 1980

Stocqueler J. *The Wellington Manual* (Calcutta) 1840

Sykes P. *A History of Persia Vol. 2* (London) 1951

Symons M. *One continuous picnic: a gastronomic history of Australia* (Melbourne) 1982

Thompson E. *Rise and Fulfilment of British Rule in India* (London)

Tyrerman C. *A History of Harrow School 1324-1991* (Oxford) 1990

Villiers A.J. *Vanished Fleets* (New York) 1931

Walker P.B *All We Inherit* (Hobart) 1968

Watson D. *Caledonia Australis* (Sydney) 1984

Journals

Alvari S. 'The Company Army and Rural Society 1780-1830' *Modern Asian Studies* Vol. 27 No. 1 (Feb., 1993) p. 147

Barua Pradeep 'Military Developments in India 1750-1850' *Journal of Military History* Vol. 58, No. 4 (Oct. 1994) pp. 599-616

Bennell A. 'Wellesley's Settlement of Mysore' *Journal of the Royal Asiatic Society of Great Britain* No. 3 / 4 (Oct 1952) pp 124-125

Brittlebank K. 'Sakti and Barakat: The Power of Tipu's Tiger' *Modern Asian Studies* Vol. 29 No. 2 (May 1995) pp. 257- 269

Brittlebank K. 'Tales of Treachery: Rumour as the Source of Claims that Tipu Sultan was Betrayed ' *Modern Asian Studies* Vol. 37 No. 1 (Feb. 2003) pp. 195-211

Cherian N.   'Spaces for Races: Ordering of Camp Followers in the
                    Military Cantonments, Madras Presidency, c. 1800-64
                    Social Scientist Vol. 32, No. 5/6 (May –June 2004)
                    p.33

Cooper R.   'Wellington and the Marathas in 1803' *The
                    International History Review* Vol. 11, No. 1 (Feb.,
                    1989) pp. 31-38

Cooper R.   'Culture, Combat and Colonialism in 18th Century
                    India' *International History Review* Vol. 27, No. 3
                    (Sept. 2005) p.545

Crowell L.   'Military professionalism in the Colonial Context: the
                    Madras Army' *Modern Asian Studies* Vol. 24 (May
                    1990) pp. 249-273

Dickinson T.   The Origins of the Synthetic Alkali Industry in Britain
                    Economica Vol. 23 No. 90 (May 1956) pp. 159-162

Ditmas, E.   'The Way Legends Grow', *Folklore,* Vol. 85 No. 3
(1974)

Devine T.   'Temporary Migration and the Scottish Highlands in
                    the 19th Century' *The Economic History Review* New
                    Series Vol. 32, No. 3 (Aug. 1979)

Fisher M.   'Excluding and Including Native of India: early 19th
                    Century Race Relations in Britain.' *Comparative
                    Studies of South Asia, Africa and the Middle East* Vol.
                    27 No. 2 2007 p.303 -314

Friedman L.   'Crimes of Mobility' *Stanford law Review* Vol. 43,
                    No. 3 (Feb., 1991) 637-658

Ford P.   'A case Study of European Training and
                    Technological Transfer in the Antebellum Period'
                    Technology and Culture Vol. 34 No. 2 (April 1993)
                    pp. 272-273

Gilbert A.   'Recruitment and Reform in the East India Company
                    Army 1760-1800' *Journal of British Studies* Vol. 15
                    No. 1 1975 pp. 91-95

Gray M.   'The Kelp Industry in the Highlands and Islands' *The
                    Economic History Review* Vol. 4 No. 2 (1951) pp.
                    200-204

Hance W.   'Crofting Settlements and Housing in the Outer
                    Hebrides' *Annals of the Association of American
                    Geographers* Vol. 41, no.1 1951 pp. 75-85

Haines R.   'Explaining the Mortality Decline in Eighteenth Century British Slave Trade' *HER New Series* Vol. 53, No. 2 May 200 pp 262-265

Hill S.C.   'The Old Sepoy Officer' *The English Historical Review* Vol. 28 No. 110 (April 1913) pp. 260-291

Jeffery B   'Martime archaeological investigations into Australian built ships wrecked in South Australia' *International Journal of Nautical Archaeology* Vol. 21 Issue 3. 1992; pp. 209-219

Jones R.   'The Plain Story of James Watt' *Notes and Records of the Royal Society of London,* Vol. 24, No. 2 (April 1970) pp. 206-211

Kingston B.   'Women in 19th Century Australia' *Labour History* No.71 (Nov. 1994) pp. 84-96

Koss S.   Wesleyanism and Empire *The Historical Journal* Vol.18, No. 1 (March , 1975) pp. 107-111

Lambton A.   'Major General Sir John Malcolm' *Iran* Vol. 33 1995 pp. 91-108

Levi J.   'Myth and History Reconsidered' *American Antiquity,* Vol. 53 No. 3 (1988.)

Mackie C.   'Traditional Housing on the Isle of Lewis' *Bealoideas* No. 74 2006 pp.71-83

McConnell F.   'New Interest in John Wesley' *The Journal of Religion* Vol. 20, No. 4 (Oct. 1940) pp. 340-358

Mahdavi S.   'Doctors, Diplomats and Missionaries in 19th Century Iran' British *Journal of Middle Eastern Studies* Vol. 32 No. 2 (Nov. 2005)

Marshall P.   'The Whites of British India, 1780-1830' *The International History Review* Vol. 12, No. 1 (Feb., 1990) pp. 26-44

Marshall P.   'British Society in India Under the East India Company' *Modern Asian Studies* Vol. 31 No. 1 1997 pp. 89-108

Mathison H   "Tropes of Well Being: Advertisement and the 18th Century Scottish Periodic Press" *Prose Studies* Vol. 21 No. 2 (1998) pp. 206-225

Minchinton W. 'Characteristics of British Slaving Vessels 1698-1775' *Journal of Interdisciplinary History* Vol. 20 No. 1 (Summer 1989) pp 53-57

Musson A.   'Origins of Engineering in Lancashire' *Journal of Economic History* Vol. 20 No. 2 (June 1960) pp. 219-220.

Nenadig S.   'The Impact of the Military Profession on Highland Gentry Families 1730-1830' *The Scottish Historical Review* Vol. 85 No. 219 (April 2006)

Palmer B.   '19th Century Canada and Australia: The Paradoxes of Class Formation' *Labour History* No. 71 (Nov. 1996) pp. 16-36

Peers D.   'Between Mars and Mammon: The East India Company and Efforts to Reform its Army' *The Historical Journal* Vol. 33, No. 2 (June 1990) pp. 385-401

Roy K.   'Military Synthesis in South Asia: Armies, Warfare and Indian Society, c. 1740-1849' The Journal of Military History Vol.69.No. 3 (July, 2005) pp.651-690

Sheridan R.   'The Guinea Surgeons of the Middle Passage' *International Journal of African Historical Studies* Vol. 14, No. 4 (1981) p.603

Steckel R.   'New evidence on the Causes of Slave and Crew Mortality in the Atlantic Slave Trade' *Journal of Economic History* Vol 46 No. 1 (March 1986) pp. 57-77

Russell P.   'The Brash Colonial: Class and Comportment in 19th Century Australia' *Transactions of the Royal Historical Society (Sixth Series)* (2002), Vol. 12: pp. 431-453

Sterns R.   'The Teredo, or Shipworm' *The American Naturalist* Vol. 20, No. 2 (Feb., 1886) pp. 131-136

Stockard J.   'Moving from Sect to Church' *Review on Religious Research* Vol. 43, No. 1 (Sept., 2001) pp. 71-74

Symes P.   'James Alexander Stewart Mackenzie: Portrait of a private note issuer' *International Bank Note Society Journal,* Volume 37, No. 1, 1998

Tolman, R.   'Treasure Tales of the Caballos' *Western Folklore,* Vol 20 No. 3 (1961)

Wilson P.   'Curse or Coincidence' *The North American Review* Vol. 230 No.1, 1930 pp. 87-92.

Wright D.   'Sir John Malcolm and the Order of the Sun and Lion'
              Iran Vol. 17, 1979 pp. 137-138
Xinhui Liu   'History: translation or Recording of the Facts' *Asian
              Social Science* Vol. 5, No. 8 Aug. 2009 pp 3-11

'Quackery in Relation to Eye Diseases' *The British Medical
Journal* Vol. 1 no. 3194 (March 1922)

Theses

Hooper B.   'Peter Degraves, Pioneer Industrialist' Honours
              Dissertation, University of Tasmania, 1969

Dillon M.   "Convict Labour and Colonial Society in the
              Campbell Town Police District: 1820 – 1839"
              unpublished Ph.D. Thesis, University of Tasmania,
              2008.

Websites (By Subject)

Henry   Ellis
http://books.google.com.au/books?id=UN4sAAAAIAAJ&pg=RA2-
PR4&dq+SIR+Henry+ELLIS   (*The Annual Report of the Royal
Asiatic Society* 17th May 1856 p.5)

John Rennie
www.britannica.com/EBchecked/topic/498171/John-Rennie

Macintosh & Degraves Silver Shilling
www.australianstamp.com
www.sterlingcurrency.com.au

Mary Reibey
http://abonline.anu.edu.au/biog/A020327b.htm
http://acms.sl.nsw.gov.au/search/simplesearch/aspx?creatorauthorartis
t&ID=2015 (Mary Reibey Journal)

Patricia Clancy 'Tasma'

www.Unimelb.edu.au/index.php/explorations/article/view/182/0
(P. Clancy 'Tasma- A Woman Novelist of Colonial Men- and 'Continental' Men. *Explorations*, No. 30 University of Melbourne.)

Peter and Ann Degravers
www.sharedtree.com/

Siege of Seringapatam
www.lib.mq.edu.au/digital/seringapatam
www.heritage-history.com
www.kashifiat.wordpress.com

William Nicholson
www.britannica.com/fact/5/152052/William-Nicholson
Oxford Dictionary of National Biography Nicholson, William (1753-1815)
www.msnucleus.org